Better Homes and Gardens®

COUNTRY BAZAAR CRAFTS

© Copyright 1986 by Meredith Corporation, Des Moines, Iowa.
All Rights Reserved. Printed in the United States of America.
First Edition. Second Printing, 1986.
Library of Congress Catalog Card Number: 85-73116
ISBN: 0-696-01560-9 (hard cover)
ISBN: 0-696-01562-5 (trade paperback)

BETTER HOMES AND GARDENS. BOOKS

Editor: Gerald M. Knox
Art Director: Ernest Shelton
Managing Editor: David A. Kirchner
Copy and Production Editors: James D. Blume,
    Marsha Jahns, Rosanne Weber Mattson,
    Mary Helen Schiltz

Crafts Editor: Jean LemMon
Senior Crafts Books Editor: Joan Cravens
Associate Crafts Books Editors: Sara Jane Treinen,
    Judith Veeder

Associate Art Directors: Linda Ford Vermie,
    Neoma Alt West, Randall Yontz
Assistant Art Directors: Lynda Haupert,
    Harijs Priekulis, Tom Wegner
Senior Graphic Designers: Jack Murphy, Stan Sams,
    Darla Whipple-Frain
Graphic Designers: Mike Burns, Sally Cooper,
    Brian Wignall, Kim Zarley

Vice President, Editorial Director: Doris Eby
Executive Director, Editorial Services: Duane L. Gregg

President, Book Group: Fred Stines
Director of Publishing: Robert B. Nelson
Vice President, Retail Marketing: Jamie Martin
Vice President, Direct Marketing: Arthur Heydendael

Country Bazaar Crafts
Crafts Editors: Joan Cravens, Judith Veeder
Copy and Production Editor: Marsha Jahns
Graphic Designer: Sally Cooper
Electronic Text Processor: Donna Russell

Cover project: See page 7.

CONTENTS

FOLK-ART FAVORITES

TO MAKE BY THE BATCH

Now's the time to start planning your next bazaar and finding the right items to make your sale a success. In *Country Bazaar Crafts* you'll find wonderful projects—all designed with country flair. Craft them singly or by the batch using a variety of techniques. And don't overlook these make-and-sell projects as gift ideas for those hard-to-buy-for people on your gift list.

Hearts and flowers—handpainted or stenciled—transform plain-Jane jars and ordinary baskets into special containers for your bazaar. Sell them "as is" or use them to package baked goods, potpourri, or other treasures. And what more down-home way is there to store (or package) recipes than in a box crafted of simple wooden yardsticks? Instructions begin on page 12.

FOLK-ART FAVORITES

Another favorite motif—this time geese—becomes a wooden accent, *left,* and struts across the appliquéd kitchen towels, *opposite,* and the calico pot holders, *below.* For a whimsical accessory to match the pot holders, stitch and stuff a goose, then nest her inside a kitchen whisk.

Inexpensive to make, pot holders are high-profit items that are always popular with bazaar shoppers. Be sure to include a stack of them stitched from traditional quilt-block designs, such as the nine-patch pattern, *opposite.*

FOLK-ART FAVORITES

To make sprightly fabric carryalls for brown baggers, just use a paper lunch sack for a pattern. Appliqué the designs shown here (or other patterns from this book) onto the fronts of the bags.

Colorful Cathedral Window pot holders, *below,* are sure to be best-sellers.

Clever packaging can make the difference between spectacular and so-so sales at any bazaar. And few packaging ideas are as enchanting as this doll, *right*.

She's assembled from just three dish towels—wrapped, tied, and embellished with embroidery and trims. Craft the doll *without* cutting the towels and—presto! She's the perfect gift for a bridal shower, housewarming, or any occasion when you need an inexpensive but imaginative present.

Here are more quick-stitch ideas bound to appeal to bazaar shoppers—hot mitts and square pot holders. These colorful kitchen helpers also are made from linen towels, then trimmed with bright embroidered ribbons.

Old-fashioned kitchen scenes, detailed enough to call to mind the aroma of fresh-baked bread, are guaranteed favorites at a country bazaar.

All you need to make these 6x9-inch designs are bits and snippets of muslin and other fabrics, plus a little embroidery floss. Hand-stitch the appliquéd scenes to a sturdy paper backing and then frame them as desired.

FOLK-ART FAVORITES

Painted Jar Lids

Shown on page 4.

MATERIALS
Glass jars and lids
Black enamel paint; varnish;
  paintbrush
Acrylic paint in assorted colors

INSTRUCTIONS
Clean the jar lids thoroughly. Paint with black enamel. When the lids are dry, paint simple folk designs, such as hearts and flowers on them (see photograph). For a dotted effect, outline the designs using the wrong end of the paintbrush. Varnish.

Recipe Box

Shown on pages 4 and 5.

MATERIALS
5 wooden yardsticks cut as
  follows: Ten 11-inch pieces
  (front, back, and bottom);
  three 3⅜-inch pieces (front
  and side braces); six 3½-inch
  pieces (sides); two 4½-inch
  pieces (back braces); two 3-
  inch pieces (bottom brace);
  and two 3¼-inch pieces
  (dividers)
Wood stain; wood glue
Acrylic paint; paintbrush

INSTRUCTIONS
Sand ends of yardstick pieces; stain. Glue together three 11-inch lengths for the front, four for the back, and three for the bottom; glue brace pieces on the back and bottom. Let dry.
Glue together the back, front, and bottom. To form each side, glue three 3½-inch lengths together. Glue ends and center of the divider to front, back, and bottom. Varnish and let dry. Referring to photograph, paint designs on box.

Stenciled Baskets

Shown on page 5.

MATERIALS
Unfinished baskets woven with
  flat strips
Acrylic paints; paintbrush
Marking pens to match paints
Stencil paper or acetate
Stencil brushes; crafts knife

INSTRUCTIONS
Paint alternating vertical strips on baskets a solid color.
On a stencil, draw designs to fit the basket strips; cut out. Center the stencil on the unpainted basket strips; paint.

Wooden Goose

Shown on page 7.

MATERIALS
1½ feet of 1x10-inch pine
5½ inches of ⅜-inch-diameter
  dowel
Drill with ⅜-inch bit
Wood glue; acrylic paint or stain

INSTRUCTIONS
Enlarge pattern, *below;* cut the goose and a 4-inch-diameter circle (base) from pine; sand. Drill holes for dowel in base and goose; glue dowel ends and insert in holes. Paint or stain.

Geese Pot Holders

Shown on page 7.
Finished size is 8x9 inches.

MATERIALS
For two pot holders
⅓ yard of green print fabric
Scraps of red pindot fabric
  (hearts), white fabric (geese),
  and interfacing (geese)
12x18 inches of batting
1½ yards of ⅛-inch-wide
  grosgrain ribbon
Permanent yellow marker
Embroidery needle
Thread; black embroidery floss

INSTRUCTIONS
Trace patterns, *opposite*. Draw 9x10-inch hearts on right side of green print fabric; do not cut out; add ½-inch seam margins.

WOODEN GOOSE

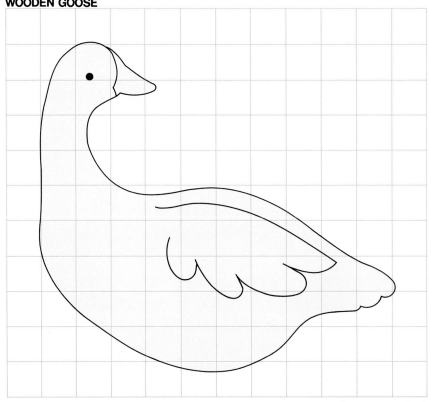

1 Square = 1 Inch

Cut out four geese and five small hearts. Referring to photograph, place the appliqués on the green hearts. Satin-stitch around the edges.

Blindstitch a tiny bow to *each* goose neck. Using six strands of floss, embroider French knots for eyes. Color the beaks with yellow marker.

Sew a folded 3-inch ribbon to the top of each pot holder for a hanger.

Cut out the appliquéd pot holders and two backings from the green print fabric. Place *each* pot holder and backing, right sides facing, atop batting; sew through all layers, leaving an opening for turning. Trim and clip seams; turn. Close opening. Topstitch ½ inch from edges.

GEESE POT HOLDERS
Full-size patterns

Cut 5

Cut 4

GOOSE TOWELS
Full-size patterns

Cut 1

Cut 1

FOLK-ART FAVORITES

Cut 1

Cut 1

Goose Towels

Shown on page 6.

MATERIALS
Plaid cotton dish towels
Scraps of gray (or black and white stripe) and orange fabrics; fusible webbing

INSTRUCTIONS
Trace patterns, page 13. Cut bodies from gray or striped fabric; cut beaks and feet from orange fabric. Cut all pieces from fusible webbing.
Fuse, then satin-stitch appliqués to towels (refer to photograph for placement).

Nine-Patch Pot Holders

Shown on page 6.

MATERIALS
Scraps of calico, print, or striped fabrics
Polyester fleece; cardboard

INSTRUCTIONS
Cut a cardboard template 2½ inches square. Cut four squares from one fabric and five from contrasting fabric. Join, using ¼-inch seams (see photograph). Cut two fleece squares and one backing piece to match top. Insert fleece between top and backing; bind edges with bias-cut strips.

Lunch Bags

Shown on page 8.

MATERIALS
For one bag
⅜ yard *each* of cotton fabric (outside) and coordinating cotton fabric (lining)
Scraps of print and solid-color cotton fabrics (appliqués)
⅝ yard of fusible webbing
⅛ yard of heavyweight fusible interfacing
Water-erasable marking pen
Pinking and straight sheers
Thread; paper lunch sack

INSTRUCTIONS
Make a pattern from a paper lunch bag by cutting down center back; cut out the bottom rectangle. Adding 1-inch seam allowance to center back of bag top and ¼ inch to the bottom rectangle, cut patterns from main fabric, lining, and fusible webbing. Cut interfacing for bottom.

Trace patterns, *opposite*. Cut appliqués from scraps and fusible webbing. Mark center front on top bag piece. Center, pin, and fuse appliqués to front of bag. Sew around appliqués with closely spaced zigzag stitches.

Fuse wrong sides of bag top fabric and lining; fuse interfacing, then lining to bag bottom.

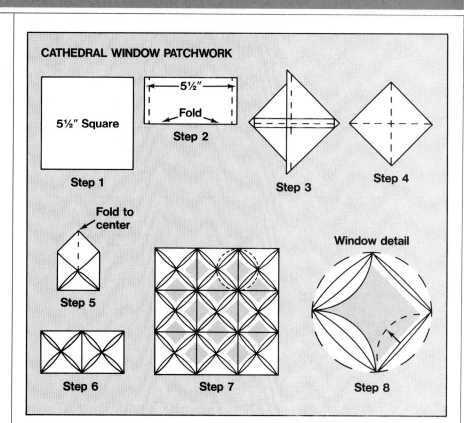

CATHEDRAL WINDOW PATCHWORK

5½" Square — Step 1

5½" Fold — Step 2

Step 3

Step 4

Fold to center — Step 5

Step 6

Step 7

Window detail — Step 8

Overlap center back with fusible webbing strip. Turn bag inside out and mark side fold lines; press. Topstitch ⅛ inch from fold lines, ending 2 inches from bottom edges. Stitch bottom piece to bag top; turn.

Fold bag to establish shape; press triangular lines (sides) inward toward lining.

Trim top of bag with pinking shears; with plain shears, cut out half-circle at top of center front.

Cathedral Window Pot Holders

Shown on pages 8 and 9.

MATERIALS
For one pot holder
⅓ yard of cotton muslin
Scraps of calico
One 8-inch square *each* of calico (backing) and quilt batting
1 yard of bias binding

INSTRUCTIONS
Refer to the diagram, *above*, to complete each step.

Cut nine 5½-inch squares from muslin. Lay one square flat (Step 1). Fold square in half; using ¼-inch seams, stitch across short ends (Step 2). Press seams open. Repeat for remaining squares.

Bring ends of seams together along open edges. Sew across remaining raw edges; leave opening for turning (Step 3). (Avoid sewing back fabric into seam.) Repeat for the remaining squares. Turn; blindstitch openings (Step 4).

Place one square on work surface, seams up. Fold and tack corners of square to center (Step 5). Repeat for remaining squares.

Hand-sew two squares together along one side (Step 6). Add another to make a row of three. Make two more rows of three squares; sew the rows together to make a 7½-inch square (Step 7).

Pin a calico square in a "window." Roll muslin edges of window over raw edges of the calico; *continued*

FOLK-ART FAVORITES

blindstitch. Sew muslin edges together at corners (Step 8). Repeat for the remaining windows. Finish the outside half-windows by blindstitching the rolled edges to muslin.

Sandwich batting between the wrong sides of top and backing. Cover raw edges with bias binding. Make a bias loop at one corner for a hanger.

Dish-Towel Doll

Shown on page 9.
Finished doll is 14 inches tall.

MATERIALS
Three dish towels
3-inch-diameter foam ball
⅔ yard of ribbon (neck)
⅓ yard of ribbon (shoes)
½ yard of gathered eyelet
Black and white felt and yarn
  scraps
Carpet thread; large needle
Stiff cardboard; glue
Small basket
Small artificial flowers

INSTRUCTIONS
To make the legs, roll one towel into a 4-inch-circumference tube; blindstitch overlap.

Thread needle with a doubled length of white yarn; knot ends and loop yarn over the center of the leg tubing, folding into two legs. Push needle and yarn up through the center of the foam ball (head), then through a small white felt circle; pull legs up under the ball. Double-knot the ends on the top of the felt circle to prevent yarn from pulling through the ball.

Center and gather the second towel over the foam ball, smoothing out the folds as much as possible. Tie with yarn beneath the head, making the neck.

For the hood and arms, roll the third towel into a tube as for the legs. Place the tube over the head, allowing the ends to hang down over each side to form arms. Tie carpet thread around the tube at neck. Sew eyelet around the top edge of hood. Tie a ribbon bow around the neck.

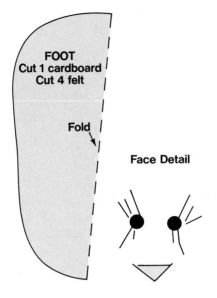

DISH-TOWEL DOLL
Full-size pattern

For hands, cut remaining eyelet into two equal parts. Roll each piece into a ½-inch-wide tube and stitch across top; insert and glue into bottom of arm tube.

Glue black yarn around face for hair. Transfer features, *above*, to face. Sew eyelashes and make two dots for the nose using one strand of black thread; sew mouth with double thread. Glue on tiny black felt circles for eyes.

Trace foot pattern, *above*, and cut from felt and cardboard; glue felt to both sides of cardboard. Glue bottom of leg to back edge of each foot. Attach the basket of flowers to the end of one arm.

Hot Mitts and Pot Holders

Shown on page 9.

MATERIALS
Kitchen towel, 18x27 inches or
  larger; thread; paper
Lining fabric (mitt); quilt batting
¼-inch-wide trim: 24 inches (pot
  holder); 16 inches (mitt)

INSTRUCTIONS
For the mitt
Trace around hand on paper, adding a 1½-inch margin. Draw around pattern twice on towel (once flopped); do not cut out.

Place atop batting; zigzag-stitch outside traced line. Trim.

To make hanging loop, cut a 1½x4-inch piece of towel fabric; fold with right sides facing and sew a ⅜-inch seam; turn.

Cut two lining pieces. Sew linings to mitt front and back across tops only, right sides facing.

Fold and baste loop to top edge of side seam on right side of one mitt piece, raw edges even. Sew mitt front to back inside zigzag stitches and ¼ inch from raw edges of lining. Leave an opening for turning. Reinforce stitching at loop; turn. Close opening; push the lining into mitt. Stitch trim around upper edge.

For the pot holder
Make a paper pattern 7 inches square. Transfer twice to towel fabric. Follow the instructions for mitt to cut out and make loop.

Baste folded loop to right side of one corner, raw edges even. Pin the pot holder together with right sides facing; stitch inside zigzag, reinforcing at loop. Trim corners and turn; close opening. Sew trim ¼ inch from outer edge.

Denim Place Mats

Shown on pages 10 and 11.
Finished mat is 11¼x15 inches.

MATERIALS
800 yards of dark blue cotton
  rug warp (for four place mats)
2 *each* of 18-inch and 26-inch
  canvas stretchers
4 metal corner braces
Flat wood shed stick and
  cardboard shuttle, each 3x18
  inches.
1½x18-inch cardboard strip;
  comb
2 pairs of worn denim jeans

INSTRUCTIONS
Assemble stretchers; reinforce corners with metal braces. Inside should measure 16x24 inches.

Knot one end of warp thread securely to top (16-inch edge) of frame, 6 inches to left of center.

Unroll the spool gradually and wind the warp around the frame (loom) for 12 inches, with 10 evenly spaced threads per inch (120 threads *each* on frame front and back). Tie end securely to frame. Loom is now warped for two place mats that are woven separately, one on each side of frame.

Weave cardboard strip into the warp near bottom of loom. The first woven rows will be against cardboard, creating a fringe when piece is removed from loom. Remove cardboard as warp tension increases during weaving; firm, even tension is necessary for the place mat to lie flat.

With shed stick, lift alternate warp threads. When 60 threads are on top, turn stick on long narrow edge, creating the shed, or weaving space.

Cut a 1-inch-deep V on each shuttle end. Wind rug warp on shuttle; pass shuttle through the shed, leaving 1 inch of rug warp hanging out. With comb, push down weft to cardboard. Remove the shed stick and repeat same step, *except* pick up the alternate warp threads (those not picked up the first time). Tuck loose end into shed.

Continue to weave with the rug warp for ½ inch, keeping edges even. Pass the shuttle through the shed, bringing it out and halfway across. Cut off carefully to avoid cutting warp threads.

Open jeans at seams, cuffs, and waistband; remove the trim and pockets; cut into 1-inch strips from cuffs to waist; cut ends at a 45-degree angle.

By hand, pass one strip of denim through shed from last pass of rug warp. Continue weaving over and under warp threads until the strip is used. Overlap ends; continue for 17 inches, pushing down each row with the comb. The last row should end about 1 inch from the frame.

Reintroduce shuttle with rug warp; weave for ½ inch. Cut off, tucking end in warp.

Weave second place mat on opposite side of loom, following directions above. When both mats are complete, cut from loom. To finish ends, knot four warp ends together, repeating to end.

Patchwork Pictures

Shown on pages 10 and 11. Finished Kitchen Stove picture is 5½x8 inches; Kitchen Cupboard picture is 5½x8¾ inches.

MATERIALS
For both pictures
¼ yard of unbleached muslin
Scraps of blue, white, brown, green, and gold fabrics
Embroidery floss to match fabrics
Sewing thread; quilt batting
Tracing paper
14-inch embroidery hoop

INSTRUCTIONS
Stitch pictures by basting fabrics for the wall and floor to a muslin backing; then add the remaining design elements.

For the cupboard picture
Trace pattern, page 19. Cut a muslin backing 1 inch larger all around than the design. Draw a line 1 inch from the edge for a finishing guide.

Place muslin in hoop. Cut wallpaper fabric ½ inch wider than top pattern on top and sides; add ½ inch to floor fabric on sides and bottom; baste onto muslin. Blanket-stitch to background using three strands of floss.

Cut remaining pieces, except cupboard worktop, to exact size. Add ¼-inch margin to cupboard worktop; cut out and turn under edges. Blindstitch details to background using sewing thread.

Using two strands of floss, satin-stitch jar lids, crock and can tops, salt and pepper shakers, sifter bottom, cupboard pulls, potatoes, and apples.

Using running stitches and one strand of floss, stitch jar rings, words on containers, sifter, and inside cupboard lines; use three strands of floss on lines around outside of cupboard doors and drawers; add two rows across the middle of basket. Make French knot knobs.

Using two strands of floss, backstitch around the cupboard, crackers, brown crock, soda, pepper, salt, flour, bowl, sifter, bag, lard, can, and basket.

Remove the design from hoop and press the raw edges to back on guideline. Using six strands of floss, blanket-stitch edges. Frame as desired.

For the stove picture
Following instructions above, trace pattern (page 18), and cut muslin, floor, and wallpaper.

Place picture in hoop. Cut stove piece to match pattern; blanket-stitch using two strands of floss. Outline stove parts and add decorative lines using running stitches and one strand of floss. Use two strands of floss to make French knot oven doorknobs. For oven handle, overcast-stitch a strand of thin yarn with floss.

Cut teakettle to size; blanket-stitch to stove using two strands of floss. Add details in satin and running stitches as desired.

Add ¼-inch margin to dress, sleeves, and apron. Add batting under dress and sleeves. Turn edges under; blindstitch in place using sewing thread.

Attach the apron in the same manner, omitting stuffing. For apron tie, cut fabric ¾x8 inches; press in half lengthwise. Turn under the edges and blindstitch. Tie in bow; tack to apron.

Cut shoes to the exact size. Using two strands of floss, blanket-stitch to the picture; outline and decorate with running stitches.

For hair, wrap six inches of floss into a ¾-inch-diameter bun; add batting underneath. Sew to head with one strand of floss. Wind six strands of floss around bun; sew in place.

Add ¼ inch to memo slate; turn under edges; blindstitch in place. Cut and attach notepad as for memo. Add memo details with running stitches and two strands of floss; make the hanger and a French knot for nail.

Cut wood box and woodpile to exact size; blanket-stitch in place.

Finish as for Kitchen Cupboard picture. Frame as desired.

FOLK-ART FAVORITES

PATCHWORK PICTURES
Full-size patterns

COUNTRY CHEER

FOR HEARTH AND HOME

Country-bred home accessories lend cozy warmth to any room. If your favorite craft is stenciling, patchwork, stitchery, crochet, or tinwork, you're sure to find a project in this section to contribute to your next bazaar—and to make for yourself as well.

Punched tinwork is a staple of the country-look crafts so popular today, and it's among the easiest to do. The 10x14-inch Home-Sweet-Home plaque, *opposite*, is made in this pioneer technique. The Courthouse Square patchwork pillows, *above*, are simple enough for a beginner to piece with ease. Directions for all the projects begin on page 28.

The hearth may be the heart of the country home, but the table is often the center of down-home hospitality. And pretty table linens can make any occasion festive. Here are three place mats designed to please guests *and* bazaar shoppers.

The crocheted ring-of-flowers design, *opposite*, is reminiscent of a country garden. Create it in cotton yarn using the colors shown, or change the color scheme to match a particular set of dishes.

The silhouette of a duck decoy, stitched in wool plaid and khaki fabric, decorates the place mat *above, right*. A three-dimensional decoy shape anchors the napkin ring.

Cotton wrapping twine from the dime store is all you need to crochet the elegant place mat *below, right*. Work the design in rows of single crochet stitches, then trim the edge with a decorative border of shells.

Soft colors, such as pastels, are so easy to live with that they never go out of style. Combine them with stenciling, stitchery, or crochet to make these appealing accessories for the bedroom and bath.

Crocheted hearts, *above,* filled with potpourri, make sweet sachets for drawers and closets. Trinket boxes, *below,* feature insets embroidered with hearts and flowers.

Two popular motifs—tulips and a coordinating leaf border pattern—grace the stenciled linens and boxes, *opposite.*

COUNTRY CHEER

Inspired by two American classics—rag rugs and patchwork quilts—these bazaar projects are sure to bring buyers to your booth.

The 48x60-inch rag-rug afghan, *right,* consists of five panels crocheted in afghan stitch. Use knitting worsted yarns in 13 colors to crochet two 12-inch-wide and three 7¾-inch-wide panels. Join the panels, then edge the afghan with three rows of single crochet.

For a larger or smaller throw, simply adjust the width, number, or length of the panels.

To approximate the varying colors found in traditional rag rugs—and make your afghan every bit as dynamic as the best of these classic area rugs—change yarn colors randomly between the first and second halves of each row. For wider stripes, simply work a single color across and back an entire row, or for several rows.

Chintz pillows, pieced in a Log Cabin design or in vertical and diagonal stripes, are colorful companions to this unusual afghan.

Simple squares and triangles brighten the pillowcases, *below.* Use our patterns, or your own favorites, to customize linens for your bazaar.

Punched-Tin Plaque

Shown on page 20.
Finished size, including frame, is 10x14¼ inches.

MATERIALS
One 9x12-inch piece *each* of aluminum and ¼-inch hardboard; scrap of plywood
Black paint; paper towels
Nail set; finishing nails
Purchased frame (or to make frame: ¼- and ¾-inch-thick pine, scraps of leather and leather lacing, wood stain)

INSTRUCTIONS
Trace pattern, *opposite*. Tape to aluminum; place atop plywood and use nail set to punch holes.

With black paint, coat aluminum; remove the excess with paper towels, leaving a light finish. Paint hardboard black; let dry.

Trace pattern for the frame top, *below,* flopping at center. From pine, cut a 1⅛x8-inch piece for the bottom and two 1⅛x14⅛-inch pieces for the sides. Dado the ends, if desired; stain.

Place punched aluminum atop hardboard backing; glue and nail the frame to edges.

Cut a 1⅜x12¼-inch piece of ¼-inch-thick pine for the stand; drill a hole 1 inch from bottom of one short end. Place other short end under center top frame piece and staple the edges together with a 1⅛x1¼-inch piece of leather.

Cut a 7½-inch length of leather lacing and insert one end through the hole on the stand; knot end. Knot the other end and staple to the bottom of frame.

Patchwork Pillow

Shown on page 21.
Finished size is 15 inches square.

MATERIALS
½ yard of 45-inch-wide blue print fabric
¼ yard *each* of 45-inch-wide solid white and dotted white fabric
15-inch-square pillow form
Water-soluble marking pen
Cardboard (templates); thread

INSTRUCTIONS
Note: Use ¼-inch seams. Cut templates to finished size; trace outlines on *wrong* side of fabrics, adding ¼-inch seam allowances.

Cut one template 2x6 inches and two templates 2x2 inches. Set one square template aside. Cut the remaining square in half diagonally; use one half for large triangle. Cut remaining large triangle in half; use one piece for template for small triangle.

From blue, cut four rectangles, eight squares, and a 15½-inch

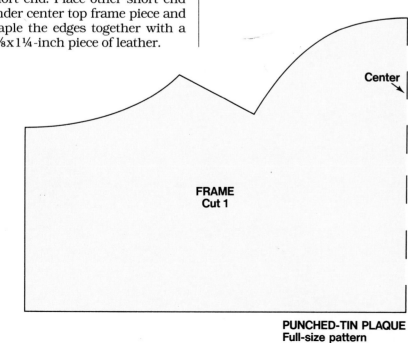

FRAME
Cut 1

Center

PUNCHED-TIN PLAQUE
Full-size pattern

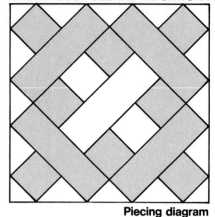

COURTHOUSE SQUARE PATCHWORK

Piecing diagram

square for the back. From dotted white fabric, cut one rectangle, two squares, 12 large triangles, and four small triangles.

Piece pillow front, following diagram, *above, right.* For borders, cut 2½-inch strips from white fabric; sew to pieced front. Sew the pillow front to back, leaving one side open. Turn; insert pillow form, and sew opening closed.

Ring of Posies Place Mats

Shown on page 22.
Mat is 13½ inches in diameter.

MATERIALS
For two mats
Lily "Sugar 'n' Cream" Cotton Yarn (125-yard balls): 1 ball *each* of white (MC), hunter green (A), light blue (B), and delft blue (C)
Size G aluminum crochet hook

Abbreviations: See page 30.
Gauge: Main motif is a 12-inch-diameter circle.

INSTRUCTIONS
CENTER MOTIF: With MC, ch 7, join with sl st to form ring.
Rnd 1: Ch 3, work 23 dc in ring, join to top of ch-3. *Rnd 2:* Ch 4, dc in same place as join, * ch 1, sk 2 dc, in next dc work dc, ch 1, and dc; rep from * around; end ch 1, join to third ch of beg ch-4.
continued

PUNCHED-TIN PLAQUE
Full-size pattern

Center

Rnd 3: Sl st into next ch-1 sp, ch 3, in same sp work dc, ch 1, and 2 dc; * sc in next ch-1 sp, in next ch-1 sp work 2 dc, ch 1, 2 dc; rep from * around; end sc in last ch-1 sp, join to top of beg ch-3.

Rnd 4: Sl st in each st to next ch-1 sp, ch 3, in same sp work 2 dc, ch 1, and 3 dc; * sc in next sc, in next ch-1 sp work 3 dc, ch 1, and 3 dc; rep from * around; end sc in sc, join to top of beg ch-3. Fasten off.

FIRST FLOWER: With B, ch 6, join with sl st to form ring.

Rnd 1: Ch 3, in ring work 6 trc, 3 dc, 6 sc, and 2 dc. Join to top of ch-3 at beg of rnd. Fasten off B.

Rnd 2: Join C in same st as join, ch 5, * sk 2 sts, sc in next st, ch 4; rep from * around; end sk 2 sts, join to first ch of beg ch-5—6 ch-4 lps made.

Rnd 3: (In next ch-4 lp work hdc, dc, 4 trc, dc, hdc) twice; in next ch-4 lp work sc, 6 dc, and sc; (in next ch-4 lp work 5 sc) twice; in next ch-4 lp work sc, 6 dc, and sc; join to first hdc. Fasten off.

SECOND FLOWER: Work as for First Flower through Rnd 2.

Rnd 3: With C (in next ch-4 lp work hdc, dc, 4 trc, dc, hdc) twice; in next ch-4 lp work sc, 3 dc, sl st in center st of corresponding petal of First Flower, in same ch-4 lp work 3 dc and sc. Complete rnd as for First Flower. Fasten off.

Work rem six flowers as for Second Flower, joining in same way to make ring; join last petal of last flower to corresponding petal of first flower to close ring.

JOINING FLOWER RING TO CENTER: Join A to any sc on last rnd of Center Motif, ch 3, **holding back last lp of each dc, work 2 dc in same place as join, yo and draw through all lps on hook—beg cluster (cl) made;** * ch 1, join with sl st between 2 sc of petals (those having 5 sc in each petal) on flower ring; ch 3, sc in next ch-1 sp of Center Motif, ch 3, working through back lps only insert hook through st before joining of same flower and in stitch before joining of next flower, pull lp through and complete sl st; ch 2,

Abbreviations

beg	begin(ning)
ch	chain
cl	cluster
dc	double crochet
dec	decrease
grp	group
hdc	half-double crochet
inc	increase
lp(s)	loop(s)
MC	main color
pat	pattern
rem	remaining
rep	repeat
rnd	round
sc	single crochet
sk	skip
sl st	slip stitch
sp	space
st(s)	stitch(es)
tog	together
trc	treble crochet
yo	yarn over
*	repeat from * as indicated

sc in first ch of ch-3, sc in side of sc in the ch-1 sp; ch 3, **holding back last lp of each dc, work 3 dc in next sc of Center Motif, yo and draw through all lps on hook—cl made;** rep from * around, end ch 3, join to top of beg cl. Fasten off.

LEAF INSERT—*Note:* Insert is worked between the tops of each flower; see diagram, *above, right.*

Beg at top edge of a flower and working counterclockwise, with A, ch 5, join with sl st in third st of right-hand petal (1), ch 4, sl st in first ch of beg ch-5; ch 4, join with sl st between next two petals (2); ch 4, sl st in same first ch of beg ch-5; ch 4, join with sl st to st where two flowers join (3); ch 4, sl st in beg ch-5; ch 4, join with sl st between next two petals (4); ch 4, sl st in beg ch-5; ch 4, join to third st of same petal (5); ch 4, sl st in beg ch-5. Fasten off.

Work insert leaf in sp between each flower—8 leaf inserts made.

EDGING: Join MC in center ch of a leaf insert, ch 3, 2 dc in same ch; * ch 2, 3 dc in same st as leaf

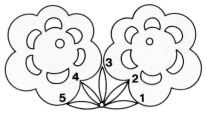

Assembly diagram

insert joining on next petal, ch 2, 3 trc in sp between next 2 large flower petals, ch 2, 3 dc in same st as next leaf insert joining, ch 2, 3 dc in center ch of next leaf insert, rep from * around; end ch 2, join to top of beg ch-3.

Last rnd: Sl st in next dc, ch 3, 4 dc in same dc; * sc in next ch-2 sp, work 5 dc in center st of next 3-dc grp; rep from * around; end sc in last ch-2 sp, join to top of beg ch-3. Fasten off.

Duck Place Mats

Shown on page 23.
Finished size of *each* place mat is 12½x18 inches.

MATERIALS
For 2 place mats, napkins, and napkin rings
1 yard of 44-inch-wide solid-color cotton-blend fabric
¾ yard of 44-inch-wide plaid wool-blend fabric
Two 14x19-inch pieces of thin batting
20 inches of ¼-inch-wide grosgrain ribbon
Four 60-mm gold beads (eyes)
2 ounces of polyester fiberfill

INSTRUCTIONS
For the napkin ring
Trace pattern for small duck, *opposite;* add ¼-inch seam allowance. Cut from plaid fabric. Join with right sides facing, leaving opening. Clip curves, turn, and stuff lightly; close opening. Hand-sew beads in place for eyes.

Cut a 3x6-inch rectangle from plaid fabric. Press under ¼ inch on narrow ends.

Fold in half lengthwise with the pressed edges out and right sides facing. Sew long edges together using a ¼-inch seam allowance. Turn; press with seam running down middle of strip.

With seam to inside, join into loop; slip-stitch to back side of duck. Cut a 10-inch ribbon and tie a bow around duck's neck.

For the place mat

Trace large duck pattern, *below*. From wool plaid fabric, cut two 3x15-inch strips (A) and two 3x10-inch strips (B). From solid-color fabric, cut four 3x3-inch squares (C), one piece 10x14¾ inches (D), and one piece 14x19 inches (E).

Using ¼-inch seams, sew the pieces together (right sides facing), in the following order: Long sides of A to long sides of D; C to ends of B; B/C to ends of place mat top.

Turn under and press ¼ inch around edges of duck. Center on place mat top and baste in place.

Lay backing fabric (E), right side up, atop batting; lay appliquéd place mat top, right side down, atop backing fabric. Sew

backing, batting, and top together ½ inch from edge; leave open at bottom edge. Turn; close opening.

Sew around duck and inner rectangle of place mat using medium-wide zigzag stitches. Press.

For the napkin

Cut a 14-inch square. Turn under edges ¼ inch twice; stitch.

NAPKIN RING
Cut 2

PLACE MAT
Cut 1

DUCK PLACE MATS
Full-size patterns

Crocheted String Place Mats

Shown on page 23.
Finished size is 14x18 inches.

MATERIALS
For one place mat
Cotton wrapping twine (352-yard ball or equivalent yardage), available in most hardware stores
Size G aluminum crochet hook or size to obtain gauge below

Abbreviations: See page 30.
Gauge: 8 sc = 2 inches; 10 rows = 2 inches.

INSTRUCTIONS
Ch 63. *Row 1:* Sc in second ch from hook and in each ch across, ch 1, turn—62 sc.
Row 2: Working in *back* lps only, sc in each sc across; ch 1, turn. *Rows 3–46:* Rep Row 2.

EDGING: *Rnd 1:* Working under *both* lps, in first sc work sc, ch 2, sc—corner made. * Sc in next 60 sc; in last sc work sc, ch 2, sc. Work 44 sc evenly spaced along next side to corner. In corner st work sc, ch 2, sc; rep from * for rem 2 sides (do not work last corner); join with sl st to first sc.
Rnd 2: Sl st into ch-2 corner sp, ch 1, in same corner sp work 2 sc, ch 2, 2 sc. Sc in each sc around and work 2 sc, ch 2, 2 sc in each ch-2 corner sp; join to first sc.
Rnd 3: Sl st in next sc and into ch-2 sp; ch 2, in same sp work 2 hdc, ch 2, 3 hdc. * Ch 1, sk sc, hdc in next 3 sc; rep from * 16 times; ch 1, sk last sc, in corner sp work 3 hdc, ch 2, 3 hdc. Continue around as established, ending ch 1, sk last sc; join to top of ch-2.
Rnd 4: Sl st in next 2 hdc and into ch-2 sp; ch 4, in same corner sp work 10 trc. * (Sk 3 hdc, sc in next ch-1 sp, sk 3 hdc, 7 trc in next ch-1 sp) 8 times; sk 3 hdc, sc in next ch-1 sp; 11 trc in corner sp. Rep from * along next side, working between ( )s 6 times.

EMBROIDERED HEART-MOTIF BOXES
Full-size patterns

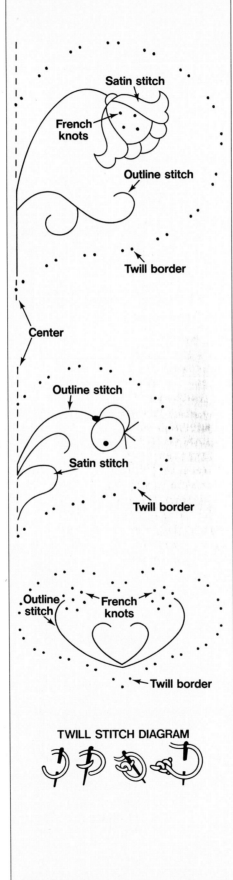

Satin stitch

French knots

Outline stitch

Twill border

Center

Outline stitch

Satin stitch

Twill border

Outline stitch

French knots

Twill border

TWILL STITCH DIAGRAM

Work rem 2 sides to correspond, ending sc in last ch-1 sp; join with sl st to top of ch-4.
Rnd 5: Ch 1, sc in same st as join. Sc in next 5 trc; **ch 4, sc in last trc made—picot made.** Sc in next 5 trc. * Sc in next sc and in next 4 trc, work picot, sc in next 3 trc. Rep from * 7 times more; sc in next sc, sc in next 6 trc, work picot, sc in next 5 trc, sc in next sc. Work rem sides as established; join with sl st to first sc; fasten off. Weave in all ends; press with steam iron.

Embroidered Heart-Motif Boxes

Shown on page 24.

MATERIALS
Embroidery floss in light and dark pinks, yellow, medium blue, and several shades of green
10-inch square of white fabric
Wooden Shaker boxes with insert lids
Scraps of ¼-inch foam, batting, or fleece
1½ yards *each* of ⅝-inch-wide white satin ribbon and ⅛-inch-wide pink-and-blue-striped grosgrain ribbon
Embroidery hoop; glue
Antique furniture finishing oil
Water-soluble marking pen

INSTRUCTIONS
Trace patterns, *left,* onto white fabric with water-soluble marking pen, allowing space around each design to fit box lids; do not cut out.
Place fabric in hoop. Use six strands of floss to embroider designs, referring to photograph for color placement. To complete the twill-stitch borders, refer to diagram, *left.*
Lightly sand boxes; apply a coat of finishing oil.
Iron the fabric with right side down. Trim to fit insert. Glue to insert with a layer of foam, batting, or fleece between. Place inserts in lids. Tie ribbons around the boxes.

Stenciled Bed Linens And Boxes

Shown on page 25.

MATERIALS
Bed linens (or make projects
   from commercial patterns)
Wooden boxes of various sizes
Stencil paint and brushes
Stencil and tracing papers
Cardboard; sandpaper
Utility knife
Decorative trims for pillows
Varnish or oil for boxes
continued

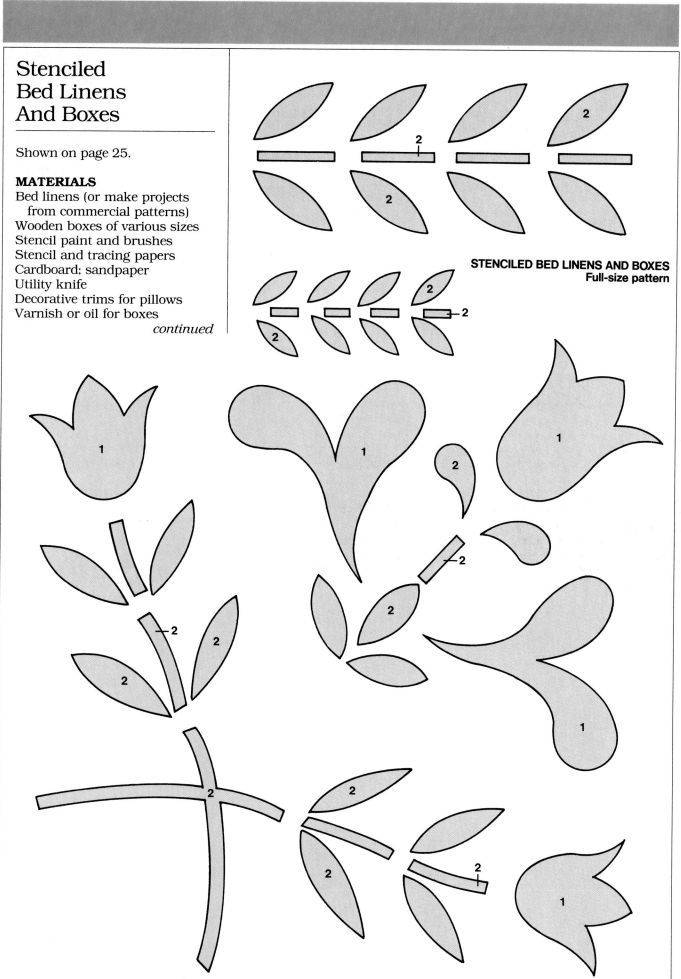

STENCILED BED LINENS AND BOXES
Full-size pattern

INSTRUCTIONS

Trace designs, *page 33*. Glue to cardboard. Lay stencil paper atop patterns; cut out motifs. On one stencil cut designs marked 1; on the second stencil cut designs marked 2.

Referring to photograph for design ideas, tape stencil to projects. Following paint manufacturer's directions, paint designs using stencil brush. Let each area dry before painting adjacent areas. To set colors, follow manufacturer's instructions.

For wooden items, lightly sand edges. Apply a coat of oil or varnish, if desired; let dry. Tape stencils in place; paint using acrylics.

Crocheted Heart Sachets

Shown on page 24.
Finished size is 4x4½ inches.

MATERIALS
DMC Cébélia crochet cotton, Size 10 (1 ball will make several ornaments)
Size 6 steel crochet hook or size to obtain gauge given below
Polyester fiberfill
⅔ yard of ⅛-inch-wide ribbon for *each* sachet

Abbreviations: See page 30.
Gauge: 9 dc = 1 inch.

INSTRUCTIONS

Ch 4. *Row 1:* 4 dc in fourth ch from hook; ch 3, turn. *Row 2:* 3 dc in first dc; ch 1, sk 1 dc, dc in next dc, ch 1, 3 dc in top of turning ch; ch 3, turn—2 ch-1 sps.

Row 3: 3 dc in first dc, ch 1, sk 1 dc, dc in next dc, (dc in ch-1 sp, dc in dc) twice; ch 1, sk 1 dc, 3 dc in next dc; ch 3, turn.

Rows 4–7: Work 3 dc in first dc, ch 1, sk 1 dc, dc in next dc, dc in ch-1 sp and in each dc; dc in ch-1 sp and next dc; ch 1, sk 1 dc, 3 dc in last dc; ch 3, turn.

Row 8: Dc in 3 dc, ch 1, dc in next 21 dc, ch 1, dc in next 3 dc;

ch 3, turn. *Row 9:* Dc in 3 dc, ch 1, dc in next 9 dc, (ch 1, sk 1 dc, dc in next dc) twice; dc in next 8 dc, ch 1, dc in 3 dc; ch 3, turn.

Row 10: Sk first dc, dc in next 2 dc, dc in ch-1 sp, ch 1, sk 1 dc, dc in 6 dc, ch 1, sk 1 dc, dc in next dc, dec in next ch-1 sp and dc as follows: Yo, draw lp in first st, yo, draw through 2 lps (2 lps rem on hook), yo, draw lp in next st, yo, draw through 2 lps (3 lps rem on hook), yo, draw through 3 lps; ch 3, turn.

Row 11: Sk first dc, dec over next dc and ch-1 sp, dc in next dc, (ch 1, sk 1 dc, dc in next dc) twice; ch 1, dc in ch-1 sp; dec over next 2 dc; ch 3, turn. *Row 12:* Dc in each st and ch across. Fasten off.

SECOND SIDE—*Rows 1–9:* Work same as above. *Row 10:* Attach thread in center dc of Row 9, ch 3, dec over ch-1 sp and next dc, ch 1, sk 1 dc, dc in 6 dc, ch 1, dc in ch-1 sp, dc in next 2 dc; ch 3, turn.

Row 11: Sk 1 dc, dec over next 2 dc, dc in ch-1 sp, (ch 1, sk next dc, dc in next ch) 3 times; dec over next ch-1 sp and dc, ch 3, turn.

Row 12: Dc in each st and ch across. Fasten off.

EDGING—*Rnd 1:* Join thread in center of heart at top of Row 10; ch 5, sl st in top of Row 11, ch 5, sl st in top of Row 12, (ch 5, sk 2 dc, sc in next dc) 3 times; (ch 5, sc in top of next row) 11 times; ch 3, make 2 dc in tip of heart, ch 3, sc in top of next row, (ch 5, sc in top of next row) 11 times; (ch 5, sk 2 dc, sc in next dc) 3 times; ch 5, sl st to top of Row 11, ch 5, sl st to top of Row 10.

Rnd 2: Sl st to center of first lp, (ch 5, sc in next lp) around to point, ch 3, dc in point, ch 3, sc in next lp, (ch 5, sc in next lp) around, sl st to center of first lp.

Rnd 3: (Sc, hdc, dc, **ch 2, sl st in top of dc—dc picot made;** hdc, sc) in each lp around to ch-3 lp, dc picot in next dc, (hdc and sc) in ch-3 lp at point; (sc and hdc) in ch-3 lp, dc picot in next dc, (hdc and sc) in ch-3 lp; (sc, hdc, dc picot, hdc, and sc) in each lp around. Fasten off.

ASSEMBLY: Place two hearts together. Beginning at top center, weave ribbon through Rnd 2 of edging, leaving an opening for stuffing. Add fiberfill, and continue weaving ribbon to top; tie bow.

Rag-Rug-Style Afghan

Shown on pages 26 and 27.
Finished size is 48x60 inches.

MATERIALS
Brunswick Germantown Knitting Worsted (100-gram skeins), or an equivalent amount of worsted-weight yarn: 2 skeins each of 4233 Hurricane, 4020 Light Mulberry, 4661 Light Denim Heather, 4033 Teal, and 4142 Light Wisteria; 1 skein each of 4163 Dark Spruce, 4183 Light Oriental Rose, 441 Ripe Berry, 403 Light Yellow, 425 Maroon, 4362 Medium Ochre, 40154 Pale Terra Cotta, and 444 Dartmouth Green
Size 8 afghan crochet hook or size to obtain gauge
Size H aluminum crochet hook
Blunt-end tapestry needle

Abbreviations: See page 30.
Gauge: 9 sts = 3 inches.

INSTRUCTIONS
Note: Afghan consists of two 12-inch-wide and three 7¾-inch-wide panels. Work colors randomly thoughout. Large stripes are made by repeating same color

for more than one row. Change colors on left side of work.

SMALL PANEL (make 3): With afghan hook and any color yarn, ch 35.

First Half of Row 1: Leaving all lps on hook, sk first ch, * insert hook in next ch, yo, draw up lp; rep from * in each ch across—35 lps on hook.

Second Half of Row 1: Yo and draw through first lp on hook, * yo, draw through 2 lps on hook; rep from * until 1 lp rem on hook.

First Half of Row 2: Insert hook under *second* vertical bar of Row 1, yo, draw up lp and leave on hook; * insert hook in next vertical bar, yo, draw up lp and leave on hook; rep from * across row to within 1 bar of end; insert hook under last bar and thread behind it, yo, draw up lp—35 lps on hook.

Second Half of Row 2: Rep Second Half of Row 1. Rep Row 2 (first and second halves) until 155 rows are completed.

Last row: Draw up lp under second vertical bar and draw through lp on hook; * draw up lp in next vertical bar and draw through lp on hook—1 lp on hook; rep from * across to within 1 bar of end; insert hook under last bar and thread behind it, draw up lp and draw through lp on hook; fasten off.

LARGE PANEL (Make 2): Ch 54 and work as for 3 small panels, *above.* Block panels.

EDGING: With Hurricane, sc around *each* panel, working 3 sc in each corner st; join with sl st to first sc. Fasten off.
Sew panels tog, placing Large Panels between Small Panels.

BORDER: *Rnd 1:* With wrong side facing, sc in each sc around entire afghan, working 3 sc in each corner st. *Next 2 rnds:* Change to teal and rep Rnd 1. Fasten off.

FINISHING: Weave in all loose ends. Steam lightly.

Chintz Pillows

Shown on page 27.
Pillows are 15 inches square.

MATERIALS
½-yard lengths of assorted colors of chintz in purples, pinks, blues, yellow, and gold
½ yard of muslin; thin batting
2 yards of ¼-inch-thick cording for each pillow
Polyester fiberfill; thread

INSTRUCTIONS
Refer to the photograph for color placement. Use ¼-inch seams throughout.
For Log Cabin pillow
For backing fabric, cut a 16-inch square from muslin; baste a 2½-inch chintz square at center.
Cut 1½-inch-wide chintz strips and piece around center square, following diagram, *below,* and referring to photograph for color placement. Trim pillow front to 15½ inches square. Cut a chintz pillow back and batting to correspond. Place pieced top over batting and sew close to edges.
Cover cording and baste to pillow front. Pin the pillow back to front, right sides facing. Stitch, leaving an opening. Turn, stuff, and sew opening closed.

For striped pillows
Cut strips of varying widths (from 1¼ to 2½ inches), at least 24 inches long for the diagonal-stripe pillow and 16 inches long for the vertical-stripe pillow.
For the diagonal-stripe pillow, join strips until pieced fabric is

LOG CABIN PILLOW

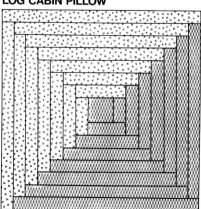

large enough to cut a 15½-inch square with the stripes running diagonally. For the vertical-stripe pillow, sew strips together; cut a 15½-inch square.
Cut batting and chintz backing to match fronts. Make cording strips and finish as for Log Cabin pillow.

Patchwork Pillowcases

Shown on page 26.

MATERIALS
Purchased pillowcases
Cardboard (templates)
Tracing paper
Assorted fabric scraps

INSTRUCTIONS
Trace patterns, *below;* cut from cardboard. Adding ¼-inch seam allowances, cut squares and triangles from fabric. Referring to photograph for placement, turn under raw edges and appliqué to the pillowcase hems. Finish with a narrow (1-inch-wide) bias-cut border appliquéd in place.

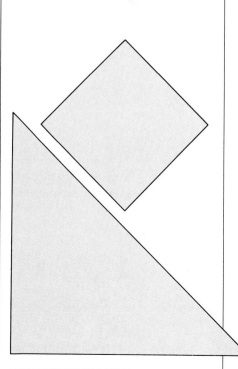

PATCHWORK PILLOWS
Full-size patterns

BRIGHT BEST-SELLERS

FOR THE CHILDREN'S CORNER

No bazaar would be complete without a booth full of gifts for babies and children. Here are playthings, trims for youngsters' rooms, and even a batch of kid-pleasing projects for parents.

With crisply starched apron and cap, this nanny doll, *right*, is a charming accent for an infant's nursery. She and her tiny charge are created from gray T-shirt fabric, and their faces are shaped by a technique called needle-sculpting. Bead babies, *above*, stitched from hankies and lace, make perfect trims for shower gifts, or even a newborn's first Christmas tree. Directions begin on page 46.

BRIGHT BEST-SELLERS

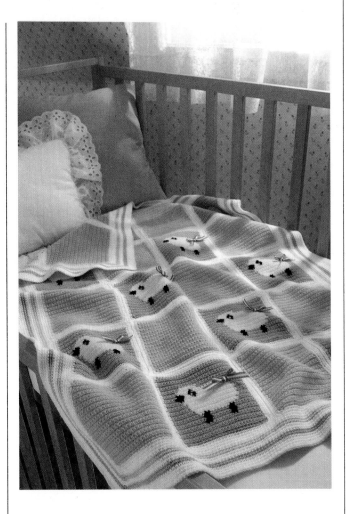

Babies and toddlers love soft, pretty afghans as much as parents do. And these two crocheted designs are sure to be a hit at your next bazaar.

The heart coverlet, *left,* measures 36 inches square. A stand-up border of soft shells edges each of the filet crochet hearts. The sheep afghan, *right,* crocheted in fine baby yarn, is 27x34 inches.

Simple toys such as the bunny and chick, *above,* make colorful, huggable additions to any baby's crib.

Patterned after the yellow pencils familiar to schoolchildren everywhere, the throw rug, *above*, is sure to brighten any boy's or girl's room.

Rows of just one stitch—single crochet—make up the rug, and simple shaping techniques form the point. Worked in acrylic rug yarn, it is machine-washable and -dryable.

Dressed in her Sunday best, this country lass, *opposite*, will win any little girl's heart. Our 13-inch-tall doll features an embroidered face and a soft yarn hairdo. An easy-to-piece patchwork pinafore spruces up her old-fashioned calico prairie dress.

For strong, smooth seams that enhance the appearance and durability of your dolls, trace *stitching* lines onto the *wrong* side of one piece of fabric (one arm, one leg, and so forth). Place fabric pieces together (for legs, arms, and body) and sew seams *twice,* using short stitches.

Finally, trim the fabric ⅛ inch beyond the seams, making sure the seam allowances are uniform in width.

BRIGHT BEST-SELLERS

There weren't any rockets in pioneer days, but nowadays even kids who love country decor are fascinated by space-age designs and toys. The crocheted rug and wooden climbing toy, *left,* are just the ticket for junior astronauts who like lively, up-to-the-minute accessories and playthings in their rooms.

The rug measures 22x30 inches. The companion toy, crafted of 1-inch-thick pine, measures 8 inches tall.

Bread dough crafts are always popular at bazaars. And this unusual—and colorful—clown, *below,* is a guaranteed winner, for parents as well as kids. Unlike most pint-size dough ornaments, this cheerful fellow is 11½ inches tall, the perfect size for a wall or door decoration.

BRIGHT BEST-SELLERS

When you're crafting bazaar projects for kids, you'll want to include some designs that will charm their parents as well, such as the bibs and blackboard shown here.

These practical kid coverups, *above,* are made from scraps of fabric and lace. Fabric appliqués also trim the 7½x9½-inch sitter information slate, *right.*

Sitter Info:

9 11

ABC

What pre-schooler—and mom or dad—wouldn't be thrilled with this high-flying bear? A tape measure, sewn to one balloon's ribbon, turns this charming patchwork teddy into a growth chart.

The embroidered barrette holders, *above,* are designed to hang on the wall. They'll keep a youngster's hair clips close at hand.

Nanny Rabbit

Shown on page 37.
Finished size is 12 inches high.

MATERIALS
For the Nanny
9¼-inch length of ¼-inch-
diameter wooden dowel
¾x2x2½-inch wooden block
12-inch-long pipe cleaner
Gray T-shirt knit fabric: 3x12
inches (head); 3x10 inches
(both arms); 3x3 inches (ears)
Scraps of pink satin
Two 4-mm black beads
White carpet thread
Pink pearl cotton thread
Powdered rouge
Fiberfill; glue
For the Baby
3x7½ inches of gray T-shirt knit
(body) and 8-inch square of
pink knit fabric (blanket)
Scrap of pink satin
2 tiny black beads (eyes)
Pink embroidery floss; fiberfill
10-inch piece of ¼-inch-wide
satin ribbon
For the Nanny's clothing
¼ yard *each* of dress, apron, and
nylon net fabric
1⅛ yards of narrow lace (dress)
⅓ yard of wide lace (apron)
½ yard of ⅛-inch-wide ribbon
(dress)
Pink embroidery floss
4½ inches of narrow eyelet (hat)

INSTRUCTIONS
For the Nanny
FOR THE BODY: Trace pattern
pieces, *right*. With right sides facing, fold head fabric in half to
measure 3x6 inches. Lay pattern
on fold (with fold at top); draw
around shape. Sew on line, leaving an opening; trim and turn.
Stuff head. Draw ¾-inch-diameter circles (cheeks) on sides of
center front seam, beginning ¼
inch below beginning of seam.
Insert needle and carefully pull
fiberfill into each cheek. Backstitch around each circle through
both fabric and fiberfill, using
one strand of thread. Backstitch
under chin (see diagram, *above*).

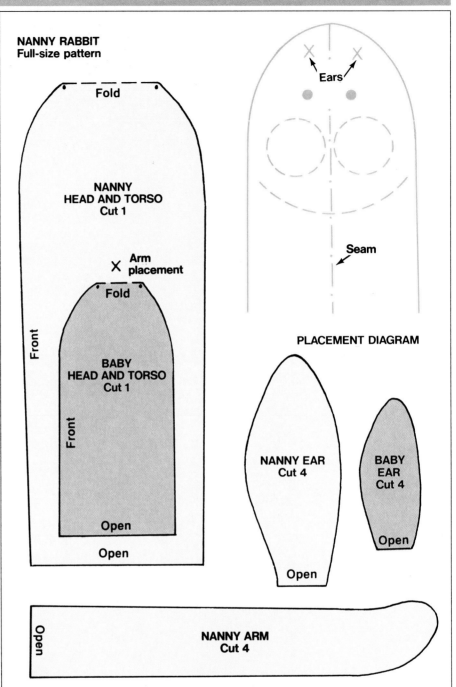

NANNY RABBIT
Full-size pattern

Fold

NANNY
HEAD AND TORSO
Cut 1

X Arm placement

Fold

Front

BABY
HEAD AND TORSO
Cut 1

Front

Open

Open

Ears

Seam

PLACEMENT DIAGRAM

NANNY EAR
Cut 4

BABY
EAR
Cut 4

Open

Open

Open

NANNY ARM
Cut 4

Satin-stitch nose with pearl
cotton (see photograph for placement). Sew on eyes. Pull thread
tightly to form bridge of nose. Pull
carpet thread through cheek area
for whiskers. Color cheeks with
rouge.
With right sides facing, pin ear
(gray) fabric to satin. Trace ear
pattern; flop for second ear. Sew
on line; leave an opening. Turn.
Fold under raw edges; close opening. Tack together lower corners
of each ear; sew ears to head.

Insert dowel into head; stop ½
inch from top of head. Firmly
stuff torso area around dowel;
tightly gather bottom edge of fabric; glue securely around dowel.
Fold arm fabric in half, right
sides facing. Draw around pattern for each arm. Stitch on line;
leave opening for turning; trim;
turn. Cut pipe cleaner ¼ inch
shorter than arm; insert; stuff
arm. Turn under raw edges ¼
inch; sew to body. Repeat for other arm.

Drill a ¼-inch-diameter hole in center of wooden block. Glue the dowel into hole.

FOR THE DRESS: Cut a 3x6-inch rectangle for bodice; fold in half crosswise (3x3 inches). To make square armholes, place fold on left; mark ⅝ inch from top edge, 1⅛ inches from fold, 1⅜ inches from right edge, and 1⅞ inches from bottom; cut out. Narrowly hem top and bottom edges; topstitch narrow lace to neckline. Slip bodice onto Nanny. Overlap back opening, turning under raw edge; topstitch.

Cut a 3x4-inch rectangle for sleeves and narrowly hem long edges. Topstitch narrow lace to one hemmed edge (bottom). Sew side seams.

Gather top of sleeve; slip onto arm. Adjust gathers and blind-stitch to bodice armhole. Gather wrist.

Cut skirt 8x25 inches. Sew the short edges, right sides facing, to 2 inches from top. Turn; narrowly hem bottom; topstitch narrow lace on hemline.

Fold netting lengthwise; sew to inside of skirt top; trim bottom. Gather top of skirt to fit Nanny's waist. Cut a 1¼-inch-wide waistband the length of skirt top plus an inch. Sew skirt to one edge of waistband, extending the band ½ inch beyond edges of skirt opening. Fold extensions toward band; turn under raw edge. Fold waistband in half; topstitch. Slip skirt onto Nanny; close opening.

FOR THE APRON: Cut apron 6½x12 inches. Mark the message on one long side of fabric, placing letters at least an inch above the edge; backstitch using two strands of floss.

Narrowly hem the short sides. Turn up bottom edge ¼ inch; stitch. Sew wide lace to bottom edge. Gather top to 3½ inches. Stitch a 1¼x4¼-inch waistband to top, extending ½ inch beyond each edge. Fold in extensions; fold band in half; press; do not topstitch yet.

Cut two 2x12-inch apron ties. With right sides facing, fold in half lengthwise. Sew diagonally across one end and across long side; turn and press. Insert and tuck *each* raw end of tie into waistband; baste. Topstitch band and ties.

Tack a narrow ribbon bow to the neckline. Fold eyelet trim into thirds; securely sew the bottom edges together; slip-stitch eyelet to the head for hat.

For the Baby

Follow instructions above for Nanny. Cheek circles should be 5/16 inch in diameter.

Diagonally fold pink knit fabric in half; wrap around baby; tack in place under one arm and to Nanny body.

Bead Babies

Shown on page 36.
Finished dolls are approximately 7 inches tall.

MATERIALS
For each doll
1-inch-diameter wooden bead (head); two ⅜-inch-diameter beads (hands)
Pipe cleaners
12-inch-square handkerchief
½ yard of ⅛-inch-wide ribbon
½ yard of 1¼-inch-wide flat lace (optional)
¼ yard of white fabric (body)
Polyester fiberfill
Embroidery floss (hair)
Acrylic paints; glue

INSTRUCTIONS
FOR THE DOLL: From white fabric, cut two 3x5-inch pieces for body. Sew together with ¼-inch seams, right sides facing; leave one short end open. Turn; stuff lightly.

Cut a 5-inch length and a 2-inch length of pipe cleaner. Fasten the shorter (neck) piece to the middle of the longer (arm) piece, making an inverted T. Insert into opening; add stuffing and hand-stitch shoulders closed.

Glue beads to the pipe cleaner ends. Paint face, referring to photograph. Glue short strands of floss to head for hair.

FOR THE CLOTHING: Cut a 3½x6½-inch paper pattern for dress front and back. On one short end, mark 1¼ inches in each direction from two corners; cut off triangles.

Cut a 2½x2½-inch paper pattern for raglan sleeve; fold in half. Measure 1¼ inches in each direction from one open corner; cut off triangles.

Cut the patterns from handkerchief, placing dress and sleeve hems on edge of handkerchief. (For plain dress, cut from white fabric. Add lace as desired.) With ¼-inch seams and right sides facing, sew sleeves to dress front and back. Sew underarm seams.

Place dress on doll. Turn neck edge to inside and gather. Gather wrists.

For lace bonnet, cut a 1½-inch-diameter circle from white fabric. Gather lace to fit; stitch to circle. Glue bonnet to head.

For plain bonnet, cut two right triangles from hankie corners, each with 3-inch sides. Stitch the raw edges together, right sides facing; turn and fold. Place on head and make two pleats at back; tack to back of dress.

Tie bow around doll's neck.

Sheep Afghan

Shown on page 39.
Finished size is 27x34 inches.

MATERIALS
Baby yarn: Two 2-ounce skeins *each* of pink and blue, three 2-ounce skeins of white and one ½-ounce skein of black
Size F crochet hook
Blunt-end tapestry needle

Abbreviations: See page 30.
Gauge: 5 sc = 1 inch; 6 rows = 1 inch.

INSTRUCTIONS
Note: Ch 1 and turn at the end of each row.

BLUE BLOCKS (make 10): With blue yarn, ch 28. *Row 1:* Sc in second ch from hook and in each ch across—27 sc.

continued

Rows 2–6: Sc in each sc.

Row 7 (right side): Sc in first 6 sc, insert hook in next sc, yo, pull up lp—2 blue lps on hook; cut a 22-inch length of black yarn, drop blue yarn, with black yarn at back of work, yo and draw through 2 blue lps on hook—color change made. Carrying blue yarn along top edge of work, sc with black over the next 2 sts, changing to blue at the end of second black st. Drop black; do not carry it along. Work 6 sc with blue, finishing last sc with another 22-inch length of black. Work 2 sc with black, carrying the blue yarn, change to blue, drop black, and complete the row with blue.

Row 8 (wrong side): Continue following chart. When making a color change on the wrong side, bring color to be dropped to the wrong side, then yo with new color and complete the stitch.

Rows 9–10: Follow the chart, *below*, for color changes, carrying blue across legs. Cut off excess black yarn at end of Row 10, leaving a 4-inch tail; weave in under black sts.

Row 11: Change to white according to chart; do not carry blue across. Tie in a second skein of blue and complete the row.

Rows 12–18: Work according to chart, untwisting skeins as necessary. *Row 19:* Tie on a 20-inch length of black where indicated on chart for snout; do not carry any yarns along under it.

Row 20: Tie on a 14-inch length of black where indicated for ear.

1 Square = 1 Stitch

Carry white along under black stitches of ear.

Rows 21–25: Work according to chart. At end of Row 25, cut off white and first skein of blue, leaving 4-inch tails. Weave in all ends.

Rows 26–31: Sc across 27 sc with blue. At end of Row 31, fasten off and weave in end.

FOR PINK BLOCKS (make 10): With pink, ch 28. *Row 1:* Sc in second ch from hook and in each ch across; ch 1, turn—27 sc.

Rows 2–31: Sc in each sc; ch 1, turn. Fasten off.

BORDER FOR EACH BLOCK— *Rnd 1:* With right side facing, attach white with sc in end of first row. Sc around block with 1 sc in end of each row, 1 sc in each st along top and bottom edges, and 3 sc in each corner; join with sl st in first sc at beg of rnd.

Rnd 2: Ch 1, sc in each sc around, 3 sc in each corner st; join with sl st in first sc at beg of rnd. Fasten off.

ASSEMBLY: Alternating pink and blue blocks, with right sides facing, whipstitch blocks together, working in *back* lps of sc along one side and under both lps of each corner st. Make four strips of five blocks each. Sew strips together in same manner.

BORDER: Work 8 rnds of sc around edge of blanket: 2 white, 2 pink, 2 white, 2 blue, and 4 white. Sc around entire blanket, working sc in each sc, 3 sc in each corner stitch. Join each rnd with sl st to beg sc. Fasten off at the end of each color, weave in all ends.

Crocheted Heart Coverlet

Shown on pages 38 and 39. Finished size is 36x36 inches.

MATERIALS
Phildar Luxe 025 (50-gram balls): 3 of white, and 2 *each* of light pink and rose
Sizes E and F aluminum crochet hooks

Abbreviations: See page 30.
Gauge: Both filet and shell motifs are 6½-inch squares (without the border). With Size E hook, 7 dc = 1 inch, 4 rows = 1 inch.

INSTRUCTIONS
SHELL MOTIF (Make 12): With white and Size F hook ch 8, join with sl st to form ring. *Rnd 1:* Ch 4, work 23 trc in ring, join to top of beg ch-4.

Rnd 2: Ch 9, trc in same st as join, * (ch 2, sk trc, dc in next trc) twice; ch 2, sk trc; in next trc work trc, ch 5, and trc; rep from * around; end ch 2, sl st in fourth ch of beg ch-9.

Rnd 3: Sl st to center of next ch-5 lp, **ch 3, work 2 dc, ch 1, and 3 dc in same ch—beg corner made;** * ch 2, dc in next trc, (ch 2, dc in next dc) twice; ch 2, dc in next trc; ch 2, **work 3 dc, ch 1, and 3 dc in center ch of next ch-5 lp—corner made;** rep from * around; end ch 2, sl st in top of beg ch-3.

Rnd 4: Sl st to next ch-1 corner sp, and work a beg corner, * ch 2, sk 2 dc, dc in next dc, (ch 2, dc in next dc) 5 times; ch 2, sk 2 dc, work corner in next ch-1 sp; rep from * around; end with dc in top of ch-3, ch 2, sk 2 dc, sl st in top of beg ch-3.

Rnd 5: Rep Rnd 4 *except* rep between ( )s 7 times.

Rnd 6: Rep Rnd 4 *except* rep between ( )s 9 times.

Rnd 7: Sl st to next ch-1 corner sp, ch 8, dc in same sp, ch 2, sk 2 dc, dc in next dc, (ch 2, dc in next dc) 11 times; ch 2, sk 2 dc, in corner sp work dc, ch 5, and dc; rep from * around; end dc in top of ch-3, ch 2, sk 2 dc, sl st in third ch of beg ch-8. Fasten off—13 sps on each side with 4 corner sps.

BORDER: *Rnd 1:* Join rose in center ch of corner ch-5 lp, ch 3, work 2 dc, ch 5, and 3 dc in same lp; * work 2 dc in each ch-2 sp to next ch-5 corner lp; in corner lp work 3 dc, ch 5, and 3 dc; rep from * around—32 dc each side of motif. Fasten off.

FILET HEART MOTIF (Make 13): With light pink and Size E hook, ch 50. *Row 1:* Dc in eighth ch from hook, * ch 2, sk 2 ch, dc in next ch; rep from *—15 sps. Ch 5, turn.

Row 2: Sk first dc, * dc in next dc, ch 2; rep from * across; end dc in third ch of turning ch-5. Ch 5, turn.

Row 3: (Dc in next dc, ch 2) 6 times; dc in next dc, **2 dc in next sp—block (bl) over sp made;** (dc in next dc, ch 2) 7 times; dc in third ch of turning ch-5. Ch 5, turn.

Row 4: (Dc in next dc, ch 2) 6 times; **dc in each of next 4 dc—bl over bl made;** (ch 2, dc in next dc) 6 times; ch 2, dc in third ch of turning ch-5. Ch 5, turn.

Rows 5–15: Continue in pat following chart, *below right,* for the heart design.

Row 16: Work 3 sps, 4 bls; **ch 2, sk 2 dc, dc in next dc—sp over bl made;** work 4 bls, 3 sps.

Rows 17–20: Continue in pat following chart. Fasten off at end of Row 20.

BORDER: *Rnd 1:* With right side facing and Size F hook, join rose in top right-hand corner sp, ch 3, 2 dc, ch 5, and 3 dc in same sp, * 2 dc in each ch-2 sp to next corner; 3 dc, ch 5, and 3 dc in corner sp; (dc in each of next 2 sps, dc in top of end st of row) 8 times; dc in each of next 2 sps; rep from * around; join to top of ch-3—32 dc each side. Fasten off.

RUFFLE: Work along outline of heart shape in center of motif. *Rnd 1:* With right side facing, Size F hook, and point of heart at top, join white in side edge of bl at point of heart design, ch 5, sl st in edge at other side of same bl, * ch 5, sk 1 bl, sl st in next bl; rep from * around entire outline of heart keeping ch-5 lps smooth and motif flat, join to first ch.

Rnd 2: Work sc, hdc, 3 dc, hdc, and sc in each ch-lp around, working only 5 sc in ch-lp at center top of heart. Join to first sc. Fasten off.

FINISHING: With a filet heart motif in each corner and alternating motifs, whipstitch motifs together to make 5 wide by 5 long.

OUTER BORDER: With right side facing and Size F hook, join rose in any corner sp. *Rnd 1:* Sc in each dc around working 5 sc in each corner sp and 2 sc in each motif joining; join to first sc.

Rnd 2: Ch 3, dc in next sc; in next sc work dc, ch 5, dc; dc in each sc around working dc, ch 5, dc in center sc of corners; join to top of ch-3—186 dc on each side. Fasten off.

Rnd 3: With Size F hook, join white in any corner sp, ch 6, dc in same sp, ch 2, * dc in next 2 dc, ch 2, sk 2 dc, (dc in next dc, ch 2) twice; sk 2 dc; rep from * to next corner sp, working dc in each of last 2 dc on side; ch 2, work dc, ch 3, and dc in corner sp; work 3 rem sides to correspond, end ch 2, join to third ch of beg ch-6.

Rnd 4: Sl st to corner sp, ch 3, work 3 dc, ch 3, and 4 dc in same sp, * dc in each of 2 dc of next 2-dc group, sk next ch-2 sp, in next ch-2 sp work 3 dc, ch 2, and 3 dc; rep from * to the next corner, end with dc in each of 2 dc of last 2-dc group; in corner sp work 4 dc, ch 3, and 4 dc; work rem 3 sides to correspond; join to the top of beg ch-3.

Rnd 5: Sl st to corner sp, **ch 5, in same sp work (trc, ch 1) 9 times; trc in same sp—corner scallop made (11 trc counting ch 5 as trc and ch-1 sp).** * sc in sp between next 2 dc of 2-dc group, **in next ch-2 sp work (trc, ch 1) 8 times; trc in same sp—side scallop made;** rep from * around

working 11 trc with ch-1 between each trc in the ch-3 sps at corners. Join to fourth ch of beg ch-5. Fasten off.

Rnd 6: Join rose in first ch-1 sp of any side edge scallop, sc in same sp, * ch 2, sc in next sp, (ch 4, sl st in third ch from hook for picot, ch 1, sc in next sp) 5 times; ch 2, sc in last ch-1 sp of same scallop, sc in first ch-1 sp of next scallop; rep from * around, working 7 picots in each corner scallop and 5 picots in each side scallop. Join to first sc. Fasten off.

Crib Toys

Shown on page 39.
Finished toys are 6 inches tall.

MATERIALS
For each toy
¼ yard of calico
12-inch square of coordinating print fabric
6 ounces of fiberfill
Embroidery floss (eyes)
Pom-pom (tail)

INSTRUCTIONS
Patterns include ¼-inch seam allowance. Sew pieces together with right sides facing, unless otherwise indicated.

For the Bunny
Enlarge pattern on page 50 and cut out. Cut and piece a 2½x30-inch boxing strip. Cut two ears *each* from calico and coordinating print fabric.

Sew ears together; leave bottoms open; turn. Pleat bottoms; pin to right side of bunny at marking, raw edges together.

Sew boxing strip to one bunny, folding in and sewing short ends. Join boxing strip to remaining bunny; leave opening. Turn and stuff; sew opening closed.

Using floss, make French knot eyes. Add pom-pom tail.

For the Chick
Make same as bunny, *except* cut boxing strip length to 22½ inches. Cut feet from coordinating fabric; stitch, turn, stuff lightly, and sew to body.

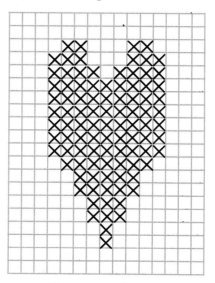

1 Square = 1 Space or Block

CRIB TOYS

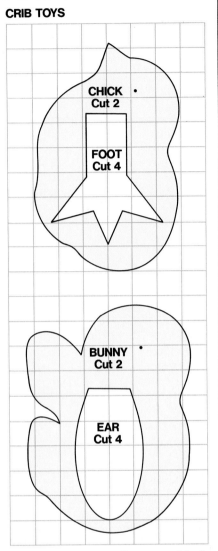

CHICK
Cut 2

FOOT
Cut 4

BUNNY
Cut 2

EAR
Cut 4

1 Square = 1 Inch

Crocheted Pencil Rug

Shown on page 40.
Finished size is 20x40 inches.

MATERIALS

Aunt Lydia's heavy rug yarn
(50-yard skeins): 170 yards of
No. 110 folly pink; 480 yards
of No. 550 sunset; 200 yards
of No. 805 white; and 100
yards of No. 825 black
Size N aluminum crochet hook
Blunt-end yarn needle

Abbreviations: See page 30.
Gauge: 4 sc = 2 inches; 5 rows =
2 inches.

INSTRUCTIONS

Note: Use a double strand of
yarn throughout. Ch 1 and turn
at the end of each row.

With pink, ch 43. *Row 1:* Sc in
second ch from hook and next 41
ch—42 sc. *Rows 2–16:* Work
even; at end of Row 16 fasten off;
turn. *Row 17:* Join white in first
sc, ch 1, sc in same st as join and
in each sc across.

Rows 18–20: Work even; fasten
off at end of Row 20; turn.

Row 21: Join black in first sc,
ch 1, sc in same st as join and in
each sc across. *Row 22:* Work
even; fasten off; turn. *Row 23:*
With white, rep Row 21.

Rows 24–26: Work even; fasten
off at end of Row 26; turn.

Row 27: With yellow, rep Row
21. *Rows 28–76:* Work even; fasten off at end of Row 76; turn.
Row 77: With white, rep Row 21.

Rows 78–92: **Draw up loop in
each of first 2 sc, yo, draw
through 3 lps on hook—dec
made.** Work across row to last 2
sc, dec over last 2 sc; fasten off;
turn. *Row 93:* Join black in first
sc, ch 1, sc in same st as join and
in next 11 sc.

Rows 94–98: Work dec over
first 2 sc, sc across to last 2 sc, dec
over last 2 sc. *Row 99:* Dec over
first 2 sc; do not fasten off; do not
turn. Ch 1, sc around entire rug
working 1 sc in end of each row, 2
sc in each corner, and 3 sc in
point of pencil; fasten off.

Using yarn needle and double
strand of white yarn, backstitch
two lines the length of the yellow
sections, dividing the width of the
pencil into thirds.

To block, steam-press lightly
with project facedown on a towel.

Barrette Holders

Shown on page 45.
Finished size is 12 inches high.

MATERIALS

⅓ yard of calico (bonnet)
¼ yard of off-white fabric (head)
4-ply yellow yarn; fiberfill
Fine-point, permanent black
    marker; blue acrylic paint
Water-soluble marking pen
Powdered rouge (cheeks)
12 inches of ⅛-inch-wide ribbon
    (to match calico)

INSTRUCTIONS

With water-soluble pen, draw a
4¾-inch-diameter circle on off-
white fabric; add ½-inch margin
and cut out. Place atop face pattern *below,* matching broken line
for the chin with bottom of drawn
line; trace features onto the face
with permanent marker.

Paint eyes with acrylic paint.
Color cheeks lightly with blush.
Cut back of head to match front.

With right sides facing, sew circles together (½-inch seam); leave
opening at top. Turn, press, stuff
lightly, and close.

For the hair, cut 18 one-yard
lengths of yarn. Align strands and
sew center of yarn bundle to top
center of head. Smooth the yarn
downward over each side; tack in
place. Braid each side and secure
ends with yarn; trim.

For bonnet, cut two 11½-inch-
diameter circles. Stitch (½-inch
seam), right sides facing; leave
opening. Clip, turn, and sew
opening closed. Gather 2 inches
from edge. Pull thread to form
bonnet top; secure. Tack bonnet
to head; adjust gathers. Add bow;
attach ribbon loop to back; hang.
Snap barrettes around braids.

BARRETTE HOLDER
Full-size pattern

Rag Doll

Shown on page 41.
Finished doll is 13 inches.

MATERIALS
For the doll
⅓ yard of muslin
Scrap of brown broadcloth
½ ounce of beige yarn
Pink and dark brown
 embroidery floss
Polyester fiberfill
For the clothing
¼ yard *each* of 45-inch-wide
 muslin (pantaloon, apron,
 apron lining) and dark blue
 calico (dress)
7 inches of ¼-inch-wide elastic
Scraps of dusty rose and pastel
 calicoes (apron)
Off-white double-fold bias tape
Scraps of medium-blue calico
 and interfacing (bonnet)
⅔ yard of ⅜-inch-wide blue
 grosgrain ribbon
½ yard lace edging

INSTRUCTIONS
For the Doll
Trace pattern, *right;* cut out.
Transfer the torso pattern and facial features to muslin. Using two
strands of floss, embroider face
(brown for eyes and brows; pink
for nose, mouth, and chin). Add
rouge to cheeks. Cut out torso
pieces. Cut arms from muslin and
legs from brown broadcloth.

With right sides facing, match
torso, arm, and leg pieces. Sew;
leave arm and leg tops, torso bottom, and shoulder seam open.
Clip; turn.

Stuff arms. With thumbs point-
ing inward, tack seam at inside
elbow to slightly crook arm. Insert arms; stitch.

Stuff body and legs. Insert and
sew legs into torso.

Cut a ¾x4⅝-inch muslin hair
guide. Wind yarn around a 12-
inch-wide cardboard until 3 inches thick. Cut yarn at ends. Center
yarn crosswise, distribute evenly
along muslin; sew along center.
Turn under ends; sew to head.
Bring several strands to front of
head (bangs); trim.

For the Clothing
All measurements include ¼-
inch seam allowances.

PANTALOON: Cut two 6½x8-
inch pieces of muslin. Sew long
sides together for 3½ inches (center front seam). For top casing,
press under ¼ inch, then ½ inch;
sew. Insert elastic and sew across
ends. Sew center back seam to
match front. For hems, press under ¼ inch; add lace; sew. Stitch
inner leg seams.

continued

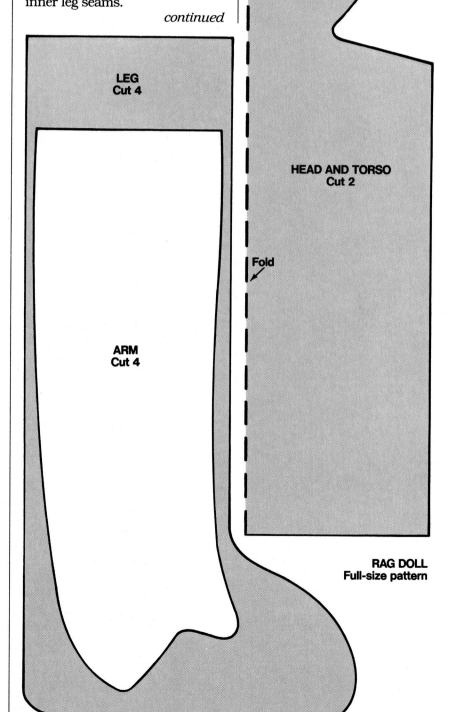

LEG
Cut 4

ARM
Cut 4

HEAD AND TORSO
Cut 2

Fold

RAG DOLL
Full-size pattern

DRESS: Cut the bodice 5¼x12 inches; cut the skirt 8½x22 inches. For bodice neck opening, cut a ¾-inch-diameter circle at center; cut a slit toward one short side (back opening). Sew around the neck; clip. Press under neckline and one back edge; topstitch.

Narrowly hem sleeves. Starting at hem, sew sleeve seams for 3½ inches; clip at end of seams.

Press under ½ inch twice on skirt hem; sew. Gather the waist and fit to bodice; match center fronts; stitch. Starting at hem, stitch 4-inch center back seam. Put dress on doll; overlap bodice back; tack. Hand-gather wrists.

APRON: Cut apron 4x9½ inches. Cut 1½x16½-inch strips of muslin and dusty rose. Join long sides, then cut crosswise every 1½ inches, making 11 two-color pieces. Alternating colors, sew a four-patch bib; join the remaining patches for bottom border.

Sew border to apron. Cut muslin lining to match; join along sides and bottom; turn. Gather waistline to 3¾ inches. For bib, cut muslin lining to match patchwork; sew together along three sides; turn. Sew fourth side to apron front, matching centers.

For waistband and ties, sew 30 inches of bias tape atop the waistline seam, matching centers; topstitch, then knot ends. For straps, topstitch the edges of two 3¾-inch lengths of bias tape. Tack to underside of bib and ties, 1½ inches from waist.

BONNET: Cut brim and interfacing, each 5x7½ inches. Cut 5-inch-square back; narrowly hem one edge. Interface wrong side of brim. With right sides facing, fold in half lengthwise. Stitch short ends; turn. Sew raw edges together; topstitch ¼ inch and ½ inch from the three other edges.

For top back, round off corners opposite hem. Starting 1 inch from the hem, gather top and sides to fit brim; stitch. Pleat center back at hemline. Tack ribbon ties to pleat and side seams.

Crocheted Rocket Rug

Shown on page 42.
Rug is 22x30 inches.

MATERIALS
Rug yarn (70-yard skein): 4 skeins *each* of red (A), medium blue (B); 2 skeins black (C) and 1 skein white (D); Crochet hook Size N (or Size 15 wooden) or size to obtain gauge
Yarn needle

Abbreviations: See page 30.
Gauge: 2 sts = 1 inch; 9 rows = 4 inches with double strand.

INSTRUCTIONS
Note: Use double strand of yarn throughout.

Beg at top of rocket with B, ch 2. *Row 1:* Work 2 sc in second ch from hook. Ch 1, turn. Hereafter, ch 1 turn at end of each row.

Row 2: Work 2 sc in first sc—inc made; inc in next sc—4 sc.

Row 3: Sc across and at same time inc 1 sc at each end of row—6 sc.

Row 4: Work even. *Row 5:* Sc across and at same time inc 1 st at beg, end, and center of row—9 sc.

Row 6: Work even. *Rows 7–16:* Rep rows 5 and 6—24 sc on last row.

Rows 17–22: Rep rows 3 and 4—30 sc on last row.

Row 23: Sc across and change to C in last sc.

Row 24: Sc across and change to A in last sc.

Rows 25–53: Work even. At end of last row change to C.

Row 54: Work even. Change to B. *Rows 55–64:* Rep rows 3 and 4—40 sc on last row.

FIRST FIN—*Row 1:* Sc in 12 sc; do not work rem sts, Ch 1, turn.

Row 2: **Draw up lp in each of next 2 sts, yo and draw through all 3 lps on hook—dec made;** sc across row.

Row 3: Work even. *Rows 4–9:* Rep rows 2 and 3—8 sc on last row. Fasten off.

SECOND FIN—*Row 1:* Join B in next sc on Row 64 (last long row worked), sc in same place and in next 15 sc—16 sc.

Row 2: Sc across and at same time dec 1 sc at each end of row. *Row 3:* Work even.

Rows 4–9: Rep rows 2 and 3—8 sc on last row. Fasten off.

THIRD FIN—*Row 1:* Join B in next sc on Row 64, sc in same place and in next 11 sc—12 sc.

Row 2: Sc across and at same time dec 1 sc at end of row. *Row 3:* Work even.

Rows 4–9: Rep rows 2 and 3—8 sc on last row. Fasten off.

FINISHING: With right side facing, join C in edge of piece and work 1 rnd of sc around entire outer edge having 3 sc in corner point at top and in each corner of fins and 2 sc in each end of Row 64, join to first sc. Fasten off.

LEFT SIDE FIN—*Row 1:* With right side facing, join D in edge at first row of A, sc in same place as join and in next 19 sc—20 sc.

Row 2: Sc across and at same time dec 1 sc at end. *Row 3:* Dec 1 sc at beg, sc across.

Rows 4–7: Rep rows 2 and 3—14 sc on last row. Fasten off.

With right side facing, join C in single crochet along outside edge between red and blue shapes and work sc along outer edge of fin with 2 sc in first corner and 3 sc in second corner. Join with sl st into rnd of C on outside edge of rocket; fasten off.

RIGHT SIDE FIN—*Row 1:* With wrong side facing, join D in edge st at first row of A and complete same as left side fin.

EMBROIDERY: Referring to the photograph, backstitch letters using double strand of C.

With rug facedown on a towel, steam-press lightly to block.

Wooden Rocket Toy

Shown on page 42.
Finished toy is 8 inches tall.

MATERIALS
One 11-inch piece of 1x8-inch
  pine
Drill with ¼- and ³/₁₆-inch drill
  bits; band or coping saw
Fine sandpaper; gesso
Acrylic paints in red, white, and
  light blue; clear sealer
12 feet of ⅛-inch-diameter rope
1-inch-tall vinyl, adhesive-back
  letters
Hook for hanging

INSTRUCTIONS
Trace patterns, *right,* and transfer to wood; cut out; sand. Where indicated, drill ¼-inch holes in hanger and ³/₁₆-inch holes in fins.

Apply gesso to rocket; let dry; sand. To paint, refer to photograph. Add letters, if desired. Apply sealer.

To assemble, fold rope in half; slip fold through center hole of hanger. Tie an overhand knot 3 inches below the fold for a hanging loop. Pull the rope ends up through holes next to center hole, then down through holes at ends of hanger. Thread the rope ends through the side fins of the rocket; knot the ends.

Bread Dough Clown

Shown on page 43.
Finished clown is 11½ inches tall.

MATERIALS
1 cup flour (not self-rising)
¼ cup salt
⅜ cup lukewarm water
Medium-gauge wire
Acrylic paints; brushes
High-gloss polymer sealer
Fine-tip permanent marking
  pen; aluminum foil

INSTRUCTIONS
Mix water and salt in a bowl. Add flour all at one time; mix well. If the dough is stiff, add more water; if the dough is sticky, add flour. Knead dough until smooth. Shape dough into a ball; store covered in a cool place.

Trace clown pattern, page 54.

Starting with a smooth round ball of dough for each part of the design, shape the pieces to fit parts of the pattern. Lay pieces atop a sheet of foil; join pieces with water.

Insert a wire loop hanger in top back of clown.

Transfer clown and foil to cookie sheet. Dry (rather than bake) in a slow oven (200 to 225 degrees) for 12 hours. Cool, then paint as desired; let dry for 24 hours. Add details with fine-tip marking pen. Apply sealer. Store in a dry place.

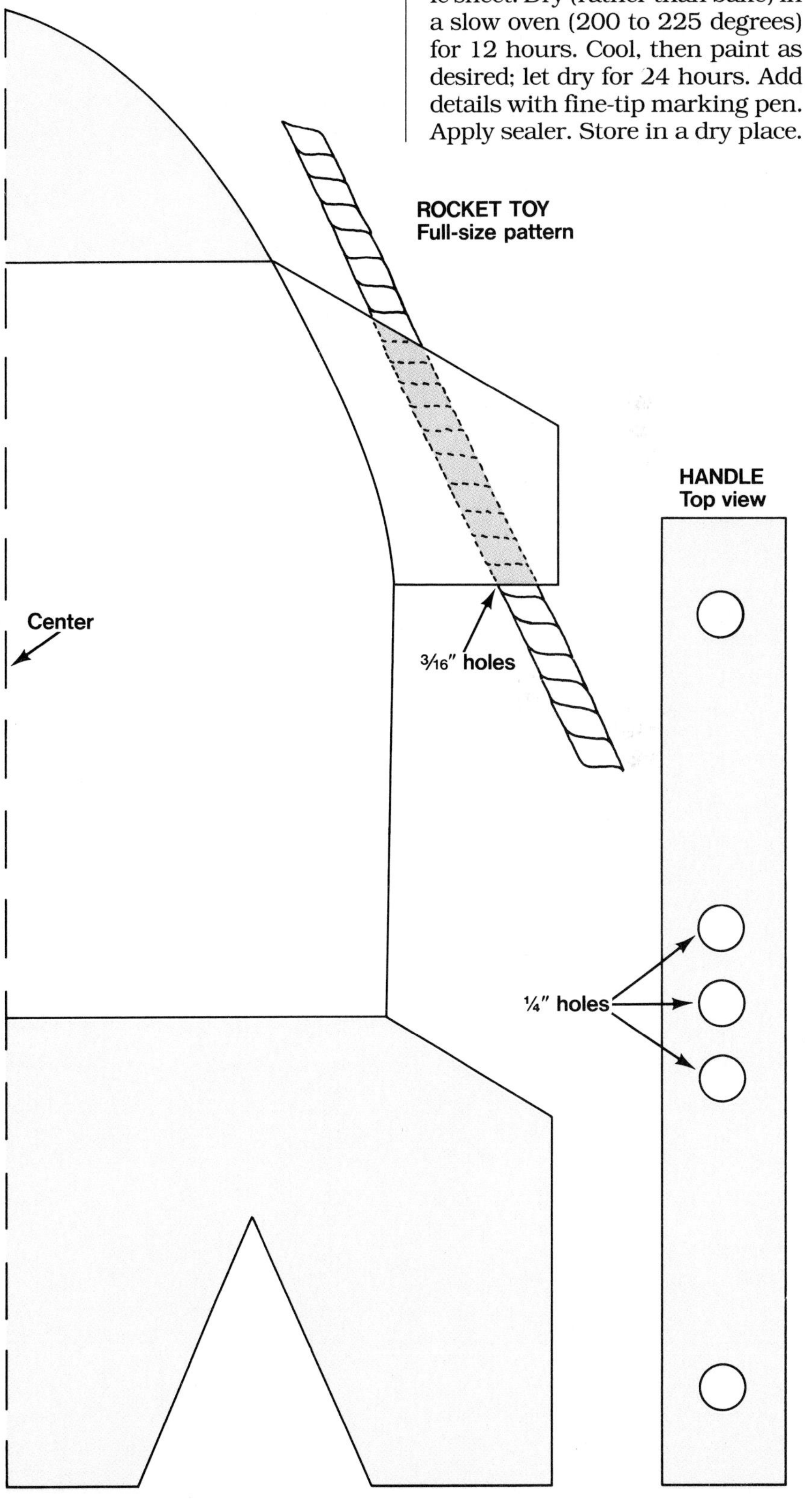

ROCKET TOY
Full-size pattern

Center

³/₁₆" holes

HANDLE
Top view

¼" holes

BRIGHT BEST-SELLERS

Fold

BREAD DOUGH CLOWN
Full-size pattern

Join patterns along dotted lines

Sitter Information Slate

Shown on page 44.

MATERIALS

Framed slate, 7½x9½ inches
Scraps of tan, red, green, yellow, white, and print fabrics
Scraps of batting and ⅛-inch-wide satin ribbon
1 yard of 1¼-inch-wide ribbon
Acrylic paints in red, black, brown, and white; brush (Size 0)
Black thread
Glue for nonporous surfaces
Drill with ¼-inch drill bit
White chalk; glue stick
Fine sandpaper
Clear sealer; stain (optional)

INSTRUCTIONS

Drill two ¼-inch holes in frame top, 1½ inches from *each* side edge. Sand; stain; apply sealer.

Trace patterns, *right*. For baby appliqué, cut two 3x4-inch pieces of calico and one of batting. Cut head and hands from tan fabric, and feet from white. Adhere to calico using glue stick.

Place batting between wrong sides of plain calico and calico piece with figure; pin together. Satin-stitch over design lines and around edges using black thread. Cut out figure outside stitching; avoid cutting threads.

Paint eyes and nose, black; hair, brown; and mouth and cheeks, red (use dry brush for cheeks). Glue ⅛-inch ribbon bow to head, just above hairline.

Cut two 2½-inch-square blocks from red and one from batting. Cut one block *each* from green and yellow fabric.

Refer to the instructions for baby appliqué to assemble the blocks. Paint letters using black acrylic. Glue appliqués to slate (see photograph for placement).

Write "Sitter Info" with chalk 1 inch below slate top; Paint over letters. Attach 1¼-inch-wide ribbon hanger to frame top.

Baby Bibs

Shown on page 44.

MATERIALS
Lace collar bib
⅜ yard *each* of blue print (bib) and ecru (lining) fabrics
Purchased ecru lace collar (or ½ yard of 2-inch-wide pregathered eyelet)
1 yard of ¼-inch-wide ecru satin ribbon
Bandanna bib
⅜ yard of denim
Red bandanna print handkerchief
Water-soluble pen

INSTRUCTIONS

Enlarge bib, flopping pattern on center line.

For lace collar bib

Cut bib from blue print *and* ecru. Cut two 1½x11-inch strips from blue print (ties). Baste collar to neckline on right side of bib. (If using eyelet, cut lace in half crosswise; hem ends. Baste *each* piece to the neckline, meeting at center front.

For ties, fold long edges to center; fold strips in half; topstitch. Knot one end of each strip. Pin unknotted strip ends at dots on right side of bib, raw edges even.

Sew lining to bib front, right sides facing (¼-inch seam); leave one side open. Avoid catching excess collar or ties in stitching. Turn; close opening.

Tack small ecru satin bow and rosette to bib. (For rosette, cut a 2-inch length of ribbon; gather one edge. Tack to bib.)

For bandanna bib

Cut out bib; narrowly hem outer edge.

Fold bandanna in half diagonally. With fold facing you, mark a point on the fold 8¼ inches from the *left* point. Also mark a point 4¾ inches on the *right* side of the *top* (center) point of the triangle (farthest away from you). Draw a line connecting the two points; cut on the line and discard right-hand side of the triangle.

continued

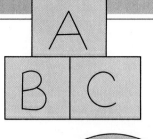

SITTER INFORMATION SLATE
Full-size pattern

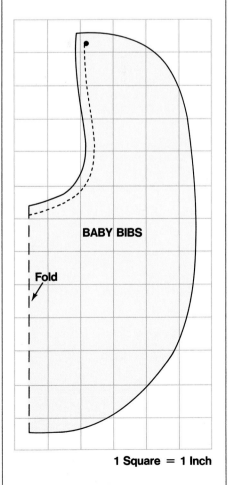

BABY BIBS

Fold

1 Square = 1 Inch

Center the unhemmed edge of the bandanna to the neckline of bib, right side of bandanna to wrong side of bib; stitch.

Turn bandanna to right side of bib. Press under ¼ inch *twice* on remaining raw edges of bandanna tie ends; sew down tie, around neck edge and back up other tie, topstitching bandanna in place. Pleat both sides of bandanna at large dot; tack.

Teddy Bear Growth Chart

Shown on page 45.

MATERIALS

½ yard *each* of red fabric (bear backing), and blue, red, and green polka-dot fabrics (balloons); ¼ yard of yellow fabric (paws, ears)
Quilt batting; measuring tape
1 yard *each* of 1-inch-wide blue, red, and green grosgrain ribbons; curtain ring (hanger)
1 yard of ⅝-inch-wide yellow grosgrain ribbon
Blue and red embroidery floss

INSTRUCTIONS

Trace pattern, *opposite*. Cut 3-inch squares from blue, red, and green polka-dot fabric. Referring to the photograph, join the squares randomly for bear front using ⅜-inch seams. Use red fabric for the bear back.

Cut out pattern, adding ⅜-inch for seams. From yellow, cut four ears and four paws. Satin-stitch paws to fronts of legs. Cut facial features from yellow; appliqué. Embroider eyes with blue floss and nose and mouth with red.

Back the front and back body pieces with batting; sew front to back, right sides facing; leave opening. Clip, turn; sew opening.

Pin ears to head front. Add batting to head front and back; sew as for body. Turn; sew opening. Sew legs in same manner. Following diagram, *below,* tack legs and head to body.

PLACEMENT DIAGRAM

Cut six balloons from polka-dot fabric (two of each color), adding ⅜-inch seam allowances. Add 2-inch hems to balloon bottoms.

Assemble balloons same as bear body, leaving bottom edges open. Turn; fold hems to inside. Tie yellow ribbon to each balloon. Sew tape measure to red ribbon; tack ribbon to each balloon. Attach ribbons to bear's left paw. Sew ring to back of red balloon.

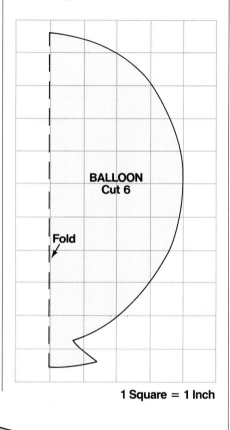

BALLOON
Cut 6

Fold

1 Square = 1 Inch

BEAR GROWTH CHART
Full-size pattern

ARM
Cut 4

PAW (ARM)
Cut 2

Fold

Fold

PAW (LEG)
Cut 2

LEG
Cut 4

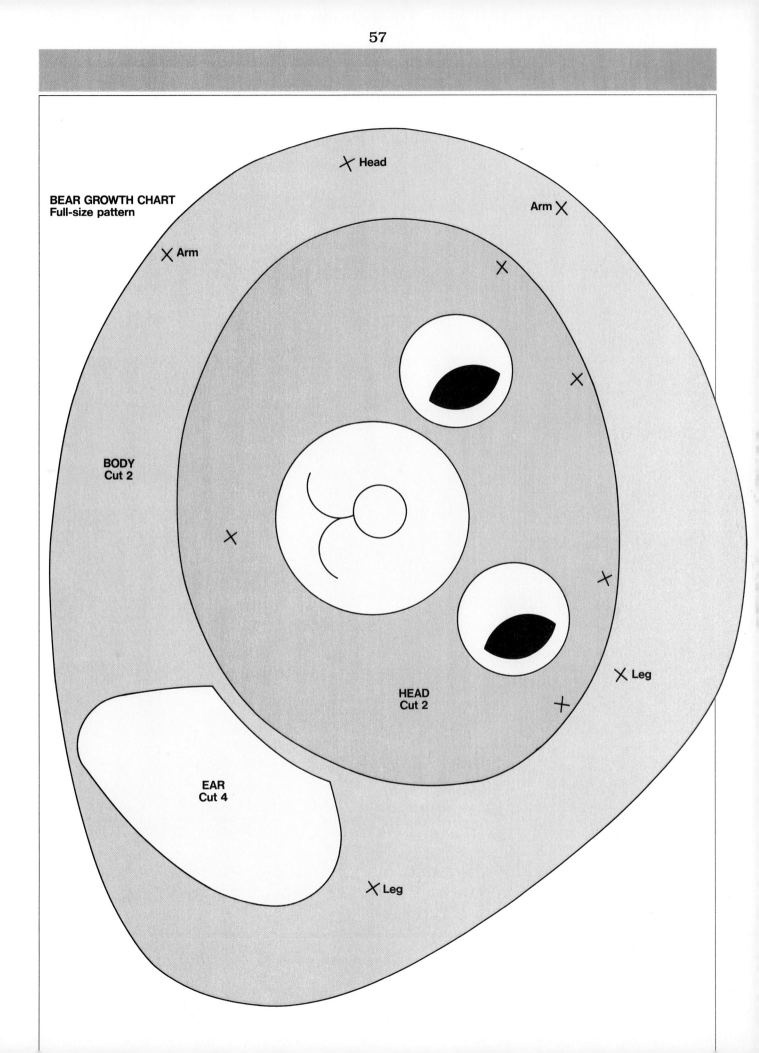

BEAR GROWTH CHART
Full-size pattern

Head

Arm

Arm

BODY
Cut 2

HEAD
Cut 2

Leg

EAR
Cut 4

Leg

SEASONAL TREASURES

Holidays and other special occasions provide the impetus *and* the theme for many successful bazaars. Gifts and trims that celebrate the season are always favorites at such fund-raisers. Whether you're planning a spring festival, a harvest celebration, or a Christmas jubilee, you'll find just the right projects to make in this chapter.

One of the nicest ways to pay tribute to spring is with loving sentiments, *left*, cross-stitched on perforated paper and assembled into cards or framed mementos. Or, craft a batch of marbleized wooden hearts, *above*, to trim a gift, a wreath, or a window. Directions begin on page 68.

SEASONAL TREASURES

What would spring be without the Easter bunny? Stitched from jogger's fleece in bright pastels, these whimsical rabbits, *left,* make fanciful gifts for any youngster's Easter basket—and playful trims for the young at heart.

Mama and papa bunny are each 20 inches tall; the babies measure 7 inches. Use beans or rice to stabilize the rabbits' bodies, so they sit securely on a table or shelf.

If you substitute embroidery or felt cutouts for the button eyes on these soft toys, the bunnies make perfect gifts for newborn babies.

Cross-stitched place cards for parties, *below,* are top sellers at any bazaar. You might want to stitch a basketful with popular names such as Becky, Tom, Susie, or Chris. Then, have a batch of *plain* cards available, and a stitcher on hand to embroider names for your customers while they wait.

Never has a more winsome fellow kept watch over a cornfield.

Dressed in country clothes, this scarecrow doll, *right,* sports raffia hair and strawlike stuffing. A round, stitched-on nose, wistful embroidered smile, and appliquéd eyes create the expression.

To make the accompanying corn shocks, gather an armload of dried grasses and other decorative material such as bittersweet. Arrange the grasses so the bottom edges align, and tie each bundle near the top with twine. Cut leaves from corn husks, and glue them and stems of bittersweet on the shocks.

Wreaths crafted of vines and twigs are perennial favorites at country bazaars. Grape stems are available everywhere. But if you have access to *other* vines that bend and wrap easily, you can create beautiful decorations from these as well.

Honeysuckle vines, prevalent in the Pacific Northwest woods, were used for the wreath, *below.* Bittersweet and a lavish bow are all you need to finish this unusual and appealing autumn decoration.

Halloween is a wonderful time to involve children in crafts. Kids can let their imaginations run free, creating costumes, masks, and games to make this holiday special.

For a fall bazaar, you might want to enlist a few young artists to help you design masks for beggars' night. Once you've machine-stitched the felt animal masks shown here—a cat, a rabbit, and an owl—you and the kids will find it easy to fabricate ideas of your own.